Lose
Love
Live

The
Spiritual Gifts
of Loss and Change

DAN MOSELEY

UPPER
ROOM BOOKS®
NASHVILLE

Upper Room Books® website: upperroombooks.com

A version of this book was originally published as *Living with Loss,* © 2007 by Dan Moseley, by Xyzzy Press. www.xyzzypress.com.

UPPER ROOM®, UPPER ROOM BOOKS®, and design logos are trademarks owned by The Upper Room®, Nashville, Tennessee. All rights reserved.

Unless otherwise indicated, scripture quotations are from the New Revised Standard Version Bible, copyright © 1989 National Council of the Churches of Christ in the United States of America. Used by permission. All rights reserved.

Cover image: Shutterstock.com
Cover design: MTW design, Nashville, TN / www.mtwdesign.net
Interior design: PerfecType, Nashville, TN

Library of Congress Cataloging-in-Publication Data
Moseley, Dan.
  Lose, love, live : the spiritual gifts of loss and change / by Dan
Moseley.
      p. cm.
  Rev. ed. of: Living with loss.
  Includes bibliographical references (p.   ).
  ISBN 978-0-8358-1043-2
  1. Consolation. 2. Loss (Psychology)—Religious aspects—Christianity. 3.
Change (Psychology)—Religious aspects—Christianity. I. Moseley, Dan.
Living with loss. II. Title.
  BV4905.3.M69 2011
  248.8'6—dc22   2010040996

To Deborah

for her faithful love and encouragement

Contents

Acknowledgments

T hanks to all who have walked with me through my life. Thanks to all those friends and family, strangers, and therapists who listened to me long enough that I woke up and discovered my life.

I am especially grateful to my colleagues at Christian Theological Seminary in Indianapolis, who gave me a place to discover myself through sharing with students the stories that shaped my ministry and life. I am grateful to all the church people, professional and nonprofessional, who invited me to talk with them about loss and its effect on growth. I am also grateful to the groups of people who were grieving losses of children and friends who invited me to share their journey. Through their grace I discovered that I was not alone.

I give thanks for my children, their partners, and my grandchildren for the contacts and encouraging words that kept me pursuing the discoveries that can come through shared losses.

I am deeply and eternally gratefully to my wife, Deborah, for her confidence in me and her patient help in encouraging me to put this out for others. Living into the life you have been given is not always easy. Deborah has been a loving and grace-filled companion to me as I have discovered my new life.

Prologue

This book is for you if you've ever lost a lover, a friend, a dog, a job, a partner, a championship game, a leg, an eye, a baby, a dream, a breast, a house, a car, a business.

It is for you if you have ever wondered what good people can do when bad things happen to them.

It is for you if your city of residence, your job, your family structure, your school, your physical ability, your beliefs, or your worldview has ever changed.

And it is for you if you have ever traveled to other cultures, become acquainted with strangers, had a baby, been betrayed, been abused, gotten married or divorced.

If any of these things have happened to you, this book is for you because this is a book about discovering new life through the losses of life.

You see, each of these events, and any other events that create a significant change in your self-understanding result in the experience of loss. Whether we choose the change or not, each change produces loss. If we marry, we lose our single life. If we become pregnant, we lose our sense of independence. If our lover dies, we lose our sense of being loved.

However, each loss is more than one thing. When we have significant changes in our lives, each loss has multiple meanings. This book is a book about the multilayered losses we experience in the living of our lives.

Moreover, this book is about what people do in the face of these changes and losses that results in some amazing and wonderful discoveries. It is about how loss is the central component in our desire to discover new dimensions of ourselves. It is about how the creation of space caused by change is exactly what is needed if we are going to become more than we have been. It is about how faith can open the spirit to the new world that is emerging.

While this book is about loss and the sadness that accompanies our losses, it is also about the discovery of more life and the excitement and adventure of that discovery. It is about the abundant life available to those who are awake and attentive to the possibilities that come to them in loss and emptiness.

However, if you are looking for a book on how you can do more to make these losses less painful or how to avoid them altogether, this book is not for you. This book assumes that loss plays a central part of being alive and that to avoid loss is to avoid life.

If you want a book that tells you "the right way" to live with and through loss, this book is not for you. If I were to tell you how to live your life in loss and then you couldn't figure out how to do what I said, your attempt would just produce guilt—and anyone who has had significant loss doesn't need someone else pointing out that he or she is doing it wrong. People who do that just make others feel more inadequate than they already feel and do not contribute to living our strength and confidence through these losses.

This book is not a list of stages or steps to follow in your journey through loss. There is no right way to do this any more than there is just one right way to live your life. Your life is unique. There is no straight line from here to there. When we think of life as a series of steps that, followed rightly, will get us what we want and prevent any pain, we start making judgments about ourselves from the beginning. If someone says we should be at stage three after four months of missing the spouse who has left us, but we are only at stage one, then we have to deal not only with our feelings but also with our guilt for not being where we "ought" to be. Among the most painful things about grieving loss are our expectations and the expectations of others that make us feel we are not "doing it right."

This book is not about doing it right. This book is about living life through its losses, an invitation to follow the scenic route through life, to pay attention to your life, to notice what is happening, and as you do, to receive it as a gift. The journey of our lives is one in which there are wanderings, roads that double back on themselves, which allow us to revisit old sites even as we wend our way toward new sights. This book is an invitation to wake up to your life, to live your life as you go, and to love your life as you experience it.

This is not a book with answers. It is a book with clues that have come from my life and the lives of people I know. Someone has said that if the path ahead is clear, it is not your path. Your life is a mystery. No one can give you all the answers. However, when we share honestly with each other, we can glean hints from one another about what might be our way.

Come with me on a journey of discovery. I will share with you what I have found in my painful experiences of loss and the joyful and graceful life that emerges through that loss. I will share with you what my friends have shared with me as we have walked together through change. I heard somewhere we read to know that we are not alone. I share with you these stories with the hope that on your journey, you will know you are not alone. I will share with you my honest experience and hope that it will illumine your path.

I invite you to open your heart up to others so that you can find fresh joy in these new discoveries. I encourage you to share your journey so that those who feel your sadness can drink from your joy as they travel with you.

"Those who want to save their life will lose it,

and those who lose their life for my sake will save it.

What does it profit them if they gain the whole world,

but lose or forfeit themselves?"

LUKE 9:24-25

Introduction: Life Is Fair

Someone once said, "Life after all is fair. Ultimately it breaks everybody's heart."[1] I would have thought I would have known this fact. After all, I spent over thirty years sharing the pain and joy of life with people in three congregations. As their pastor, I had spent countless hours walking alongside hundreds of people as they experienced all that life had to offer. I shared the agony of divorce with some of them, wept with some of them as they gave up their spouses to death, swore at the gods with some as they mourned the death of their newborn babies, descended into the depths with others as they were fired after twenty-four years with their company. I would have thought I'd have known that eventually life breaks everyone's heart.

Ironically it took more for me to get that knowledge through my thick skin. Before that could happen, I had to be stripped of the insulation that protected me from the pain and confronted with more loss and death than I could handle. It began with the discovery of cancer and, three years later, the death of my first wife, Cindy. We had been married thirty-one years. Soon thereafter, the young custodian of the church I was serving took his lover and her children hostage and, before the night was over, killed his lover and himself. Then the last of my three children married and moved out. Finally, a month later my dad died.

Up to this point, I was accomplished at facing difficulty with other people. My role as minister gave me a way of being present to the pain without it cutting so deep. But when the losses began to pile up and rip through my self-understanding as a husband, a father, and a son, I was without enough resources to keep on going.

I continued to do my work as a preacher and pastor, but I found it increasingly difficult. Speaking words of meaning became hollow. I felt like a "noisy gong and a clanging cymbal" (2 Cor. 13:2). Prayer was simply hollow ritual without meaning or power.

When I visited people in the hospital, my body cried out in rebellion. I found myself avoiding the leadership responsibilities of my job.

Finally, I chose to leave the congregation that had mentored and nurtured me and that I had served for over twenty years. I chose to leave the profession of pastor, which had sustained me and given me identity for over thirty years. I chose to leave the city in which I had discovered my skills as a minister and where I had offered them as a gift to others. I chose to lose much more after facing losses over which I had no choice.

Only then did the full effect of the losses of my life come crashing in. As I moved to a new city and became a professor at a seminary, I began to spin into chaos. As the relationships that had sustained me through the crises of my life ended, I was left naked and on my own. I could no longer avoid my feelings. I could no longer pretend that life would be the same. I discovered the terror of not knowing who I was.

I discovered raw empathy. Susan Wiltshire, in her book about her brother dying from AIDS, describes a broken heart as like a broken biscuit. When torn in half, there is twice as much surface on which to spread the butter and honey.[2] I discovered that a broken heart also has twice as much surface on which to spread the pain and grief of others. Whereas I had been able to protect my heart by playing the role of pastor, I now had no such protection. While I was able to draw on the strength that people projected on me because I was a "man of God," now I was just Dan. I had no presence to offer but my own, and the pain that others felt tore into my flesh. It was then I began to realize the truth of the statement "Life after all is fair. Eventually it breaks everyone's heart."

I found that our hearts are attached to familiar, dependable relationships and that when these change, by accident or by choice (it matters not), the heart gets ripped apart.

In the midst of this time in my life I began to reflect on my own journey—to discover if there was anything in this pain and loss that could help me understand and live life better. My heart had been ripped open, and the wounds of loss were raw. Sadness consumed me. The sharing of the Lord's Supper, where brokenness and suffering are central, became a much richer and more powerful worship experience. Shed blood and broken body became visceral, and I felt shared pain with the One remembered and with the people in the pew beside me.

I yearned for comforting, for warm light to anoint the wounds and to heal me, for the suffering to ease and for hope to visit my heart again. I wanted to believe there was light coming in through the tears of my heart, but I didn't know how to get through the pain to discover that light.

As I looked at what I was doing with my life, I grasped the truth of the poet Jack Gilbert, who said, "We must unlearn the constellations to see the stars."[3] I realized that the life I had created was no longer the life I could live. I had learned a particular way of naming reality. The people and actions of my life were constructed in a particular way, creating constellations by which I named them. The constellations were named husband, pastor, father, and son. But as life's structures disappeared, I was unable to name myself and was left looking at a black sky with millions of stars. I could no longer see the constellations—just the stars.

Dim Lights

I found myself slowing down because I didn't know who I was anymore. When I experienced the loss of my wife, my dad, my job, and the community I had called home, someone turned off the lights in my life. When you can't see very well, you don't move as fast.

The lights don't go off all of a sudden. Sometimes when one experiences a painful loss, there is a sudden burst of bright light. Sometimes when one inquires how a person is doing soon after the death of her husband, the answer may be, "She is doing amazingly well. She's taking care of business." Painful loss often produces a spurt of energy and clarity that one seldom experiences in the normal routine of life. Adrenaline rushes through our system, which insulates us from the pain and energizes us to endure the stress produced by the loss.

For most of us though that light begins to dim when our energy runs out. The energy required to deal with the immediate need to simply hold on and create some temporary stability is soon depleted. The clarity provided by the immediate tasks soon fades as the fog of unknowing descends upon us. We often find ourselves sleeping much more than we did before. The dark of sleep is much more welcoming than the light of reality that faces us.

This slowing down is very much related to the inability to see where we are going. It is very much like the descending sunset and the emerging dark of night. We find ourselves drawn to the immediacy of the present by the palpable pain of emptiness and fear. We don't want to look far ahead. We just want to rest in the present. We knew the way forward when the person we lost was still living with us, even if the way was tough. When that person is gone, we have a much harder time deciding where we are going.

Fran was married for fifteen years. Several times during her marriage, her husband physically abused her. Despite the abuse, she stayed with him because she loved him and believed the stability of the marriage was best for her and her children. She learned how to make it through most of the days and years without suffering abuse. She walked on eggshells, but she walked nonetheless. She knew if she avoided certain topics and gave in when he became angry, she would be okay.

However, one night the abuse became so brutal Fran decided she had had enough. She was terrorized by her husband, and she was terrorized by the thought of leaving her husband. But she finally found the courage to leave.

The freedom Fran felt when she left was almost as frightening as the terror of her husband. How could she live? How would she support her children? How could she be a single parent? Darkness descended, and Fran did not know what to do. The energy she had mustered to leave her husband had now evaporated, leaving Fran depressed and exhausted. She felt as if someone had turned out the lights.

Reorienting in the Dark

When the "lights go out" and we are unable to see clearly where we are going, we slow down. We sometimes stop. We try to become reoriented. Because the eyes do not pick up signals that help us know where we are, we often use our other senses. We reach out a hand, feeling our way along. We listen, trying to determine if we hear something that sounds familiar. Our sense of smell stretches up on tiptoe, trying to detect something that can give us a sense of where we are.

I remember hiking in the woods several years ago. Initially I was following trails others had made but eventually began to feel adventurous, wanting to explore unknown areas. I took off through the underbrush, sure I would come across another trail. As the sun started to set, I was hopelessly lost. I began to feel anxiety because I was losing my sight in the dimming light. There was nothing that gave me a clue as to where I was. Then I saw some deer droppings and realized that deer had been on the narrow path I was following. I also listened and heard automobile traffic in the distance. I knew the road went north and determined that I was facing west. My senses helped orient me, and I soon found my way back to the trail and returned to my car.

When it is dark, we slow down and use other senses to find our way. At this time in the journey through change and loss, we begin to understand the struggle of faith reflected in the worship of the unseen God. The apostle Paul told the people of Corinth not to lose heart because people of faith look "not at what can be seen but at what cannot be seen; for what can be seen is temporary, but what cannot be seen is eternal" (2 Cor. 4:18). When we slow down because what we have seen has disappeared, we gain insight into the power of the unseen to open up the future.

Slowing Down

When we lose someone or some activity, we slow down to a speed that feels safe. Each step is a cautious effort. Someone once told me that he had experienced the loss of his mother as a descending darkness. He said he had to live as if he were driving at night. He could only go as fast as his headlights would allow him to see.

When we have lost someone or something that has helped define who we are, remembering that we are in the dark and our eyes have to adjust can be helpful. It helps to remember that our friends may be offering a flashlight of encouragement to help us see a little farther ahead, but these are their flashlights and not ours. We see the future in the dark as only a vague outline. When driving in the darkness without lights, we have difficulty determining what is ahead of us. The uncertainty of what we see means we move cautiously, in spite of our own desire or the desire of others that we move more quickly.

Moving forward in the dark is deceptive and often confusing. Sometimes we think we see clearly, and other times we are certain we don't see anything at all. When my wife Deborah and I first started dating, we were both in free fall. Deborah was adjusting to being single after a divorce that ended a twenty-five-year marriage. I was adjusting to single life after losing my wife to death, my career to a job change, and my home of twenty years. When Deborah and I first began to date, we saw clearly and the passion was palpable. We saw clearly by the burning passion. Then one of us would become scared, and the night of uncertainty would envelop us and we would back away from the relationship. This occurred a couple of times over a three-year period. Eventually the darkness of fear and uncertainty gave way to more consistent light, and we decided to move ahead together. We began to make plans for further down the road rather than simply on the impulse of the moment. We began to wake up not only to our present feelings and fears but also to the dreams and hopes that light the path into the future.

Back Roads

I became aware that my journey of living through loss was more frequently traveled on the back roads of life. As I sorted through the emotional rubble of my life, I could not deal with the intensity of interstates and major highways. As I traveled to work from my home or to my mother's home five hundred miles away, I would choose the roads less traveled. Something drew me to the slower, less confusing route.

I then read a book that helped me understand what I was doing. Milan Kundera, in his book *Immortality*, talks of the differences between highways and roads. He suggests that highways are intended to get us from point A to point B as quickly as possible. The space between point A and point B is of little positive value. It is simply space to be passed through quickly.

Roads, on the other hand, value the space and are part of the landscape. They are designed to be traversed on foot or driven slowly. He said that before roads disappeared from the landscape they disappeared from the soul. Humans seem determined to live life always looking for it when they arrive rather than seeing the road as their life.[4]

Living with the losses of my life slowed me down and opened me to the life that is the journey rather than the life that is a destination. Kundera spoke to the deep desire I had discovered to slow down and to allow life to be lived in me. I had spent much of my life traveling from point A to point B and was living at such furious speed that I failed to notice life along the road. As I traveled the back roads of my soul, I slowly discovered rich insights into living life more fully, experiences that occur to us and that, whether we want them to happen or not, can be gifts of life to us. I realized that loss is the one of the fundamental things in life you can count on and that through loss you can discover your life.

Change and Loss

Loss is the one constant in life because change is the nature of life. Change is the one incontrovertible truth about reality. If something is alive, it is changing. And if something is changing, something is dying. I have realized that loss opens up the future in ways nothing else can. Loss makes new life possible.

This is a very difficult perspective to sell in our society, which believes that winning is everything. One of the worst things a person can be called is a loser. Our culture is enchanted with the winners, the celebrities, the people "on top." We are simultaneously cruel and callous toward those who were on top and then fell.

The message of this book—that we *lose* our way to new life—is not easy to sell. However, it is a word of truth and hope for those ordinary people who live life in its fullness. It makes sense to those who have experienced what life delivers to all—the experience of losing something that is core to who we see ourselves to be.

Mantra

I discovered how much hope this understanding offers when I was invited to speak at a national gathering. I was asked to share my spiritual journey in eight minutes. Accepting the challenge, I boiled down my life and realized that I could sum up my spiritual journey in the following mantra:

To live is to love. To love is to lose. To lose is to live.

In looking back at my life, I see that love creates life. What we love makes us who we are. If we love words, we become someone who lives with words. If we love baseball, we will spend time playing or watching it because it makes us feel alive. What we love gives us life.

We may love ourselves at a particular time in our lives. We may have loved high school. We may have loved that dress. We may have loved being a mother who nursed her baby. If we love our children, we become the type of person who is a parent to the children, and we shape our lives according to what the love of a child demands of us. If we love our job, we become a person shaped by that job. We love created things, and in loving we create ourselves.

Because we love what is not permanent, we are guaranteed to lose. Because we love what constantly changes, we will eventually lose what we know as we know it. That much is assured. We may love our job, but eventually we will lose that job—because we lose our love for what we are doing or someone more qualified may be hired or because we retire or we die doing our job. At some point, we will lose what we love; what makes us know that we are alive will disappear. To love is to lose.

The guarantee that we will lose holds true for our faith as well. Faith is a human construct. We create an understanding of our lives in relationship to God. We use symbols and language to create that understanding. These symbols, while shaped by divine power and history, are constructs of the human mind. The way we construct meaning in our lives through the symbols of our faith will change. Therefore, when we are faced with a crisis that results in losing whatever we have come to count on, the way we imagine God can also change and we may lose our faith. The object of our love is a construct of the human heart and mind. Since we constructed it, we can lose it.

We become who we are by what we love. When we lose what we love, we lose part of who we are. If our spouse walks out on us after twenty years of marriage, we will no longer be the person we were. Sometimes we have become so shaped by the way love was expressed for our partner that we lose a significant part of ourselves. Our sadness and pain is therefore as much for the loss of ourselves as it is for the loss of the other.

To live is to love. To love is to lose. But to lose is to live. If we lose one part of our life, we become open to another part. If we love having young children at home, when they grow up and leave home the empty space created by their leaving opens the door to love something else—like the freedom to travel or to visit with adults without interruption. When something disappears, it opens the space for something else.

Loss opens new space with regard to faith as well. When the way we understood God as a child no longer helps us navigate the swirling waters of adult life, we sometimes give up faith all together. For those who continue to immerse themselves in the stories and rituals of faith, new insights into the character of the Divine can emerge. When I lost confidence in the words that had been my life, I was driven into a wilderness of silence. But it was there that I realized how limited my experience of God was. I had understood God to be word. In the midst of the empty desert of silence and despair, I discovered that God is also silence—God is not only what fills space, but God is also the space that is filled. Emptiness creates space for new and expanding life.

When my granddaughter was four years old, her baby teeth began to fall out and she smiled her toothless smile. She was scared when the first one fell out, but her fear eased when she put it under her pillow and received money from the tooth fairy. Now she is proud—new teeth are coming in. She is excited about the new teeth. Her fear faded as she grew in the confidence that new teeth would replace the ones that were lost. Had she not lost those teeth, there would have been no room for new teeth. To lose is to live.

How do we learn to live with loss? How do we find the courage to embrace the empty space that creates room for new life?

Growing through Grieving

Living well through loss involvess learning how to grieve. Grieving teaches us to live again in the absence of someone or something significant. Grieving isn't just a time of unbearable emptiness and tears but a whole process of becoming a new person shaped by the memory of what is lost, not defined by it.

Grieving enables us to become a person who has experienced a divorce, not a divorced person. It enables us to become a person who has lost a partner, not a widow. It enables us to become a person who has experienced the loss of a job, not a loser. Grieving enables us to know ourselves as persons who lose something when change occurs, not as people who are losers.

Therefore grieving is a process that takes time. It is not an easy process if the loss for which you grieve represented a defining reality in your life. The amount of time grieving takes is related to the depth of the loss. When a young man loses an important basketball game, he will go through this process relatively quickly. The process helps him attend to the pain of the loss and become free of that pain, so it won't define how he plays the next game. He will be shaped by the loss but not controlled by it. A woman whose husband dies the year before he is due to retire will take longer to find the new life through this process of grieving and growing. Her identity and self-understanding have developed over a number of years, and the losses will be more complex and multidimensional.

The process of grieving involves pain because it is a birthing process, a stretching and tearing that opens the way for a new spirit to emerge. It requires the knitting together of painful and pleasant memories to discover a new way of understanding ourselves.

As I worked on this process in my own life, I did a great deal of reading and study of spirituality and growth. I came to realize that the process of grieving loss, of learning to live in the absence of someone or something significant, parallels what many religions call a spiritual pilgrimage. To grow spiritually isn't simply the practice of reading about the good ideas of others; it is about the way we process the changes in our lives, about the way we travel from death to life as we move from what is lost to what is yet to love. Spiritual growth is about living through a breaking, stretching, aching, remaking process of letting go of that which is gone and taking on a life formed in response to what is becoming.

Those who practice spiritual disciplines know that emptiness and loss are the womb for rebirth. They discipline themselves to create silence— space empty of words—in which their hearing is sharpened to hear more. In the closing of their eyes to the bright light of sight, they see what can only be seen in the dark. In the fasting from food, they experience the nourishment that comes from a hungry body. When they give alms, they learn that true wealth comes from an empty space in the wallet. When they offer hospitality, they discover the gifts of strangers who now have space in the empty chair at the table. Spiritual growth is about loss and emptiness. It is the result of space that is created when what we have trusted to hold us is not present.

Death and Rebirth

In my childhood home, words were sovereign. They were fed to me with my mother's milk. I learned to relish them and to trust them. As I learned to speak, my parents constantly reminded me how to speak correctly. They taught me that there are words that build up and words that tear down. If I used words that tore down (telling my brother he was "stupid," for instance), I paid a high price. If I used words that my mother felt demeaned the human enterprise (like "damn" or "hell"), I was required to go pick my own switch and roll up my pant legs. I became a student, and spoken and printed words fed my mind. I became a singer, and poetic words dressed in notes became my soul's food.

After the series of deaths and losses that invaded my life over a decade ago, however, words died for me. They lost their power. I lost my voice. I realized that words are like dust—cast to the wind and scattered, seldom having the lasting effect one desires.

The result was my inability to read or write. I lost the focus necessary to follow a sentence across the page and hold its meaning in my mind. I tried writing but could not develop any confidence in it.

When I spoke in public, I felt tentative—stumbling and qualifying. I came to realize that the mind in chaos has a hard time taking words into itself and ordering them into any sense. Because my mind couldn't process the way it was accustomed to, I discovered I was much more in touch with my body and my soul. My heart was also confused, and I couldn't stay in relationships very well. I realized these losses had effectively driven me out of my mind and into my body, out of my heart and into my soul.

After several years of struggle, I was surprised by a realization that freed me to put these words down on a page and send them out to others in a book. One crisp fall day, I was hiking in the forest that has become my playground and sat on a bench looking at what I call the broccoli tree. (It looks like a hundred-foot stalk of broccoli.) As the last of the late-autumn leaves drifted to the ground, I had a deep sense of sadness. I realized the words I had spoken most of my life were much like the fallen leaves. My words had fallen from my lips and turned brown. The smell of decay was in the air. Most of the words by which I had made my living had long ago disintegrated. They were not remembered, nor were they framed and put on a wall.

As I pondered this process, I settled into a deep sense of contentment. Yes, the leaves fall and die. Yes, the words fall on people's ears and die. The decaying leaves become the humus that nourishes the tree and becomes the fertile home for the gestation of new seedlings. Maybe that is what words do—they are not to live forever. They are simply designed to fall and die and silently and perpetually fertilize the new life that emerges from the earth.

As I came to this understanding, I was released from my block and decided I could write again. Then as I was relaxing in the crisp fall sun, an acorn fell and struck me right on top of my head. All the fluttering, descending leaves had spoken so gently and then suddenly, one hard little acorn dropped from nowhere and made its point. Only a few words make an impact. The rest do their work of decay and death, becoming humus for the nurturing of new life.

This book is intended to be both brown leaves and hard acorns. It is a result of the journey from trust and confidence in the life I had been given, the collapse of that life, and the emergence of new life and understanding.

In this book you will be invited to explore ten dimensions of reality we experience as we learn to embrace the new and leave the old. You will be encouraged to explore your suffering and open yourself to rebirth as the gift that comes to those who pay attention to their lives and who have the courage and patience to discover the gifts that are a part of losing, loving, and living.

As the ten dimensions of experience common to loss are identified, you are invited to recognize them in your own journey, to attend to your feelings and your thoughts as you experience them. I encourage you to slow down and explore the gifts that come through these experiences. ("A Discovery Journal" at the end of this book will help you write your way through your loss and into new life.) I believe that when you work your way through your loss in this way, you will find new parts of yourself and new resources for living a rich and vital life in the future.

In this book we will also identify persons who might be companions for your journey. When Jesus came face-to-face with his own death, he took some friends to the garden with him when he prayed. He knew that the journey through suffering and death to new life is not one that should be taken alone. As you explore your loss and hope for new life, you will want to seek out friends who can walk with you. You need several. No one person can be all things to you. Sometimes you need intimate friends; sometimes you need strangers. I have discovered that the presence of multiple companions helps us to live these experiences more fully and to discover new parts of ourselves that we might miss were we to walk alone. When you walk with others through these experiences, you can help them grow in spirit and life if you attend to some of these ways of being present with them.

Welcome to the journey. Welcome to the pilgrimage. Welcome to the discovery of life.

So out of the ground the LORD *God formed every animal*

of the field and every bird of the air,

and brought them to the man to see what he would call

them;

and whatever the man called every living creature,

that was its name.

GENESIS 2:19

1

Naming the Loss

To learn to live again in the absence of someone or something requires that one develop the ability to name that which is lost. Throughout the Bible, we have stories of humans giving names to people and to creation. The creative God gave the creative energy of naming to humans. To name something is to define its relationship to the created order. To name our losses is to begin the journey of discovering the meaning of what makes up our life.

Now, that may seem like a simple assignment. After all, when a spouse dies, what you have lost is clear. She is no longer here. She has stopped breathing. She has stopped talking. She has stopped touching. When you lose a job, what you have lost is clear. You are no longer being paid to get in your car and drive to an office and do some task that satisfies a need of some organization. When you lose a partner, what you have lost is clear. He is no longer coming home at night. He is no longer there to talk with you. He is no longer there affirming you or comforting you.

But some losses are not always so obvious. In fact, most significant losses are multilayered. Most of us are unable to name all the losses immediately. If we did, it would be so overwhelming we could not stand it. When my dad died, he physically disappeared from my life. That was about all I could deal with at the beginning. I could not talk with him on the phone. I could not hear his wry humor and his shy laughter. I could not smell his aroma. I could not call to ask for his advice.

After some time went by, I realized that I had lost a constancy I could not describe. There was an empty space that his death had created in me. I realized that I would never receive answers to some questions. I could ask my mother about what my daddy did and what he felt, but I would never really know *his* answers.

As more time passed, I realized I had lost my buffer. He was no longer there to protect me from my own mortality. I could no longer assume I would live forever because there was still someone there who would have to die first. Now he was gone. I would be next. The more time I spent without my daddy the more was revealed about the meaning of his life in mine.

Sue lost her partner in parenting. They were parents of small children. When her partner died, she was left alone. Along with the agony of an empty bed, she experienced the losses of companionship, friendship, and planning. The person whom she had bounced ideas off was not there anymore.

In time, Sue began to sense another loss. She discovered that her confidence in parenting was not nearly as strong and that she had only known herself as a partnered parent. She had never known herself as a single parent.

Her children were acting differently as well. They had never known her as a single parent, and they had never known single parenting, only the parenting that was done together. So they had lost a sense of the safety and security they had known with both parents.

Then a third loss emerged. Sue realized she didn't trust life to sustain her in the future. She saw how fragile life was, that there was no guarantee and that life can be very short. Because of this uncertainty, she found herself fluctuating between conserving everything, trying to hold on to the things she had, and spending everything since she could envision no future to save for.

When someone we love dies, we realize the future we had looked toward is gone. When we lose our vision of the future, it is hard to know what to do in the present, causing us to wonder if there is anything worth planning or living for; it all seems to come to nothing.

Sue also discovered that the music of her life with her partner was no longer being written. They had played, laughed, cried, struggled, traveled, and lived together for seventeen years. Now her partner was no longer there to contribute her music. Sue felt she was left to complete the unfinished symphony alone. She had to find some kind of resolution to the harmony and discord that had characterized the music of their lives. Writing the symphony alone, when you have always done it with another, is a difficult and fearful thing. You want to write it in a way that has the integrity of the one who is gone.

For Sue to know who she is and to learn how to live without her partner, she must continue to be open to experiencing the different losses that have occurred. Naming those losses can open her eyes to the fullness of her relationship with her partner and the multiple ways that their shared life had defined each of them. (This practice will also become a valuable resource for joy when she enters the dimension of gratitude.)

Naming the losses of our lives isn't simply the work of those who have involuntarily lost something. It happens with any significant loss, even if the loss is the natural consequence of achieving what you have desired.

Helen had been in school most of her life. She had been a good student in high school and received scholarships to an Ivy League university. She did well in philosophy and religion and decided to pursue a master's degree in theology. She loved the study of theology so much that she decided to earn a PhD and become a professor.

However, when she finally achieved her goal and received her diploma, Helen sank into a depression. She was not prepared for the losses she met with. She had known that she would miss the students she had attended school with and was prepared for that sense of loss. But she didn't realize how much more she would be losing. As she began to talk about it and live the emptiness, she discovered she had lost her sense of security. She knew how to be a student—she had been perfecting that skill for twenty years. Now she had to become a teacher and, although she had seen others teach, she didn't have the confidence in this new role that she had known as a student.

Furthermore, when she was a student, others had set the standards and rules and had defined success for her. Others had given her direction on carrying out her passion. As a teacher, she had to direct herself. She had lost the security of satisfying others even as she began to learn what she thought was her calling.

As she kept naming what this PhD had cost her, Helen realized that she no longer had her dream to motivate her. For twenty years she had been driven by the desire to earn the next degree. Her dream to get a PhD was a powerful motivator. Without that dream to energize her, she felt flat and without direction. She had doubts about whether theology was really that interesting after all.

It is important for Helen to continue exploring the different levels of loss so that she can clarify the truth about her future. She clearly loves philosophy and theology, but she had never had the opportunity to love it apart from the goal of earning a degree. A powerful part of her life's experience to this point had been a love of theology combined with a goal. Once Helen knows this, she can begin to adapt to living life in the absence of that particular goal. She can move toward naming other goals to motivate her. She may discover delight in the drive to help students learn the subjects that excite her or to fulfill a new dream of publishing her ideas for others to explore.

This process of grieving loss resembles that of taking a spiritual pilgrimage. Those who take a pilgrimage have a profound longing to experience the Divine at a holy city or shrine. That longing can be so powerful that it causes them to leave home to pursue it. One of the important things in this pilgrimage is naming what one must give up to take it. Leaving home for a long time means missing out on the experiences of those you love who stay behind. Changing your life to go on the road means you will cause stress on the family and the friends you leave, for someone must cover your responsibilities.

Moreover, when you return, you will be a new person, shaped in new ways by the experiences you have had; and they will have lost you the way you were. You will lose something of the relationship you had with others who knew you before your pilgrimage. The natural ease with which you related to your old life will be lost. Only as you are able to name the losses you will experience and as you guard against allowing those losses to control your actions will you have the courage to leave home and make new discoveries.

To grieve and grow requires noticing and naming the lived experiences of multiple losses.

Good Companions

As you journey through this early part of the process of grieving loss and growing spiritually, finding good companions to travel with you can be crucial. A fitting person for this part of the discovery is someone who is good at asking questions and can help you name the various dimensions of the loss you are experiencing.

The story of the early church as recorded in the book of Acts begins with many questions. When Jesus died, those who had followed him needed to discover the meaning of his death by naming what they had lost. They wonder with the risen Christ if his death meant the coming of the new Israel (Acts 1:6). As he ascended, the men in white robes asked them, "Why do you stand looking up toward heaven?" What did his life mean? The meaning of Jesus' life became clear only in the exploration of what his followers experience in the emptiness of his absence.

At this early stage of grieving, some people will be eager for you to see the benefits of your loss. They will constantly remind you of what you have gained. If you have had a miscarriage, they will be eager for you to know you can always try again. These folks are not helpful. At this point in the process, it is best to surround yourself with people who will let you tell your story over and over, trusting that if retelling your story is important to you, it is important to them. You need someone who not only trusts that you are smart enough to see the obvious but also realizes that it takes patience to see the more subtle and meaningful parts of this loss. Good companions are those people who don't need you to be the way you were. These individuals will allow you to be just the way you are.

Good friends are people who listen well. When we are in the midst of the collapse of a world as we have known it, we need to speak about it. No one can talk us out of our loss or pain. We must talk ourselves through our pain, our guilt, and our fear and talk ourselves into the new life growing in us. A good listener creates space for us to give voice to our loss and its meaning, and in so doing, helps us discover who we were in the journey toward who we are becoming.

Good listeners create an empty space—an empty container—that can receive the spoken losses as they pour forth, remember them, and hold them for you so that when you are able, you can come back to them and sort through them. By listening and remembering your stories, good companions can mirror them back to you when you are able to hear them and claim them. These insights will help you understand why you continue to feel sadness and help you discover the surprising richness of your lost relationships.

Any kind of growth requires giving up one thing for something else. Developing clarity about the different things you have to give up will help free you to move toward the new life, the new sense of self you desire. Naming the losses in the presence of good companions, who accept you as you are, is a valuable part of this growing process.

How long, O LORD? Will you forget me forever?

How long will you hide your face from me?

How long must I bear pain in my soul,

and have sorrow in my heart all day long?

PSALM 13:1-2

2

Feeling Pain

L earning to live again also requires that we experience the pain of the loss. This part of the process interacts closely with naming the loss. The feeling of the pain speaks to us of what we have lost. Naming those losses helps clarify the feelings. Feeling the pain helps you name more of what is lost.

Following the initial numbing shock of disbelief in the immediate experience of loss, pain presses itself into our souls and bodies. It is sometimes more than we think we can bear. We seek ways to anesthetize ourselves. It hurts too much to allow that gaping hole in our gut to bleed unstaunched. We want to feel anything other than that pain. We want to fill the empty hole within with something—alcohol, drugs, sex, sleep, work, easy love, TV. We are vulnerable to anyone who will offer us a moment's respite from that unspeakable gap within our soul.

But feeling pain is important for a number of reasons. First, it reminds us that we are alive. Following the loss of someone or something that matters deeply, our body protects us by numbing us. I remember once breaking my leg as I slipped on the ice. I got up and limped two blocks home, thinking it didn't hurt very bad. After sitting for an hour and arranging to go to the emergency room, my leg hurt so bad I could not move.

The body helps us deal with the shock of pain from physical injuries with initial anesthetic. The body performs this function for broken hearts as well. We receive help so the reality of the loss can soak in. We can't stand the truth all at once.

Eventually though, we begin to feel again and the pain sets in. The pain reminds us we are still alive and in need of healing. It will come and go, visiting us when we least expect it. When you can feel the pain of sadness and loneliness, know that this signals that you are growing stronger. When we are not strong, the body numbs us and we don't feel. If we feel the pain, we are gaining strength. Pain reminds us that something significant has happened. It reminds us that to be human is to feel. Only when we can feel the deep sadness of the loss can we ever hope to feel the deep joy of new life. Feeling is central to the ability to experience the fullness of life as it is being lived.

The Psalms are full of the agony of ancient Hebrew people as they struggled with pain and suffering. They sang their struggle, their pain, and their joy. The heart's singing helps us experience the pain we feel. The sad country songs, the traditional songs from oppressed people (such as African American spirituals), and folk songs articulate the pain and help us process it. People of faith discover comfort in singing the psalms of their ancient ancestors. This music helps us connect at a soulful level to others who have suffered and survived.

Feeling the pain also teaches us truth. When we have had a significant loss, we are tempted to live in denial. Pretending the loss has not really happened becomes an easy option. Frank was devastated when he lost his wife of forty years to cancer. Many mornings he would get up and imagine he could smell the coffee as she had begun to brew it. For a moment he would begin to speak to her as if she were in the other room. Our hearts protect us from the full truth of the loss until we can absorb it bit by bit. Feeling the pain of the loss teaches us the truth that the loss is real.

Grasping this truth is important, for it enables us to move toward the new life that is waiting for us. Until we know that the past is truly gone, we might imagine that we can live that life over again. Some people remarry soon after the death of a partner. Unless they have felt the pain and fully experienced the truth of their loss, they might try to replicate the life they have lost. They may be tempted to view their new partner as a replacement partner. The heart longs for the familiar and will try to re-create it any way possible. They want the new partner to make their life as comfortable as the lost partner had. This, of course, is impossible. Unless one is absolutely certain that the person he or she once loved is not and will never again be present to offer love, the new relationship may be a disappointment.

Living with the painful truth of absence for a significant period of time is important. Time gives the grieving person's pain the opportunity to produce more awareness of all the things that have been lost, allowing the person to name them. Just as pain in the body is a sign that something needs attention, so also pain in the heart is a sign that something still exists that we need to be mindful of.

Feeling the pain is also important for helping the body release the toxins created by suffering. The bone and sinew in the body are scarred by emotional trauma and hold the hurt well beyond the heart's ache. Tears can provide a healing release for the whole system when they are allowed to flow.

I am a white male whose culture taught me not to cry. Crying is regarded as a sign of weakness, and I was not supposed to be weak. When my first wife died, however, I was initially overcome with tears. They would not stop. Although tears are not a sign of weakness but of strength, as the demands of work and life took over, I gave up the tears. But the pain did not give up on me.

I was still experiencing many layers of loss, but I could not cry. I would just become surly and angry. I would be hard to live with. I was blue and depressed—but I did not cry. Then I saw the movie *Shadowlands* about the short life and love of C. S. Lewis and his wife, Joy. Joy died of cancer after a brief but intense relationship. That movie helped me release the tears and express my sadness. The pain eased as I was free to feel it and express it.

For several years after that, when I began to ignore my sadness and pain, I would watch *Shadowlands* and find release in my soul and body.

Tears are an important way for us to find release from the pain of our loss. Some people would advise us to give up our pain and get on with our lives. They believe the cure for grieving is just deciding that you are over it. My experience suggests that pain and sadness are not something we can choose to surrender so easily. Pain has to give up on us. Tears are a way of helping us rinse out our souls so that the sadness releases its grip on us.

Feeling the pain of loss activates the imagination for our new life. If we don't deeply feel our loss, our imagination will be reluctant to envision new ways of being. Helen, our PhD friend, had to feel the pain of the loss of pursuing her dream so that an empty space could be created for new dreams. As the old goals fade into the familiarity of normality, the new and interesting goals have the freedom to visit by way of the imagination.

Feeling pain also enables us to learn how to live anew because pain helps us notice the present. Much of our time is spent fretting and planning for the future or worrying and agonizing over the past. We spend much of our energy trying to fill the empty unknown of the future or to rethink the mistakes we might have made in the past. Pain is present and attending to it is to be focusing in the present. If we are to move beyond loss and live a new life, if we are going to notice and embrace a life coming to us in the future, we must have the ability to be alive and attentive to the present. Pain has the power to cause us to focus on ourselves. Paying attention to ourselves is an important part of the process of becoming the new person we hope to be.

I can offer one other reason to feel the pain. To feel the pain of a love lost is an indication that we have indeed loved. We seldom feel unquenchable agony when we lose something we don't love. Only our capacity to love that makes it possible to feel such deep emotional and spiritual pain. When we do not avoid the pain but embrace it, we are reminded that love is real and that we have a capacity to love—that is, to live.

Feeling pain also involves dangers. We can become addicted to it. Since pain makes us feel that we are alive, it is sometimes hard to let go of it. By remembering the loss over and over, we feel the pain, the love, and the life over and over. Sometimes the pain becomes a substitute for loving and living in the future. Sometimes it takes on a life of its own.

Many of our friends and family understandably will want to help us ease the pain. Being around deep pain as it infects people we love is hard. It is natural for us to want to fix them if we are able. This impulse to help ease the pain often tempts us to say things that are not helpful:

- "You'll be fine."
- "I know how you feel."
- "It's time to get on with your life."

Each of these statements may be true but is seldom helpful when spoken to someone overwhelmed with pain. You can allow these comments to remind you of the danger of making pain a substitute for living.

Just as losing results in pain, so spiritual growth can be painful as well. For us to grow spiritually, we must part with some things to allow room for new things to come into our lives. Our spirit is shaped by that which we love. What we love requires our time and attention. When we attend to one thing, we don't have as much time for other things. The pain of that loss must be experienced.

Jeff and Alice had been married for three years when they decided it was time to have children. Alice became pregnant, and their excitement built. The anticipated presence of a new person in the family expanded their world beyond their imagination. The birth of their child was one of the most moving experiences of their lives. Participating in the creative energy of the universe overwhelmed them with awe. The moment of birth bonded them in ways nothing else had.

As their spirits expanded in awe, their pain over the fate of babies in refugee camps dug deep in their souls. Their concern grew, and they began to raise money to provide care for those babies. As they grew in their love for their own child and for other children, however, their time spent traveling to see siblings and friends decreased. Their work for refugee babies created a dull discomfort related to what they were losing. They felt that discomfort, got in touch with their feeling, and named it. While that alone didn't heal the hurt, it at least enabled them to give themselves to their new passion wholeheartedly and not think there was something wrong with it.

Feeling pain is powerful and important for growing toward a new life when something has changed in one's life.

Good Companions

One characteristic of a good companion in this dimension of living one's loss is not being afraid of feeling one's own pain. When someone we care about is hurting deeply, we hurt as well. If a person is able to endure the feelings of pain stirred up when sharing the pain of others, that person can be a healing presence for other people when they hurt.

It is also good to be with a person who does not need to fix you. When we are feeling pain and knowing the life force through that feeling, we don't need someone to help us escape that feeling. As uncomfortable as it might be, feeling pain is something that helps us know we were loved and cared for. We don't want to lose that feeling too quickly, because we will feel more alone when it goes away. No one can save us from our pain. He or she might distract us for a while (and that can be a gift), but our pain is our own business.

Being around people who do not need us to be feeling well all the time; being with a counselor or confidant or friend, who does not like to see us in pain but who does not need to hurry us through it so they might feel better; being with people who can be present to the pain and help us see what we might learn from it—such people, who know we are strong and that, given enough time and feeling, we will grow through the experience, are invaluable companions for this journey.

A good companion for you while you are feeling pain is also someone who can just be quiet and hold your hand. Pain is selfish; when we feel it deeply, we need someone who can let us be where we are and not expect us to give of ourselves for his or her well-being.

Having friends who are simply present is helpful, because when we are numb, we often feel disconnected from the strength of the community we have known. The steadfast presence of someone who just shows up from time to time reminds us that we still belong, even if we don't feel like it. It reminds us we are remembered, even if we don't want to remember.

Often the best friends in this time are old ones—people who know you well enough and are tender enough to help you gently come out of yourself from time to time. Old friends know your pain because they have shared your life. They know what the loss means to you. Because they have lived with you, their presence reminds you of the presence that has been lost.

This kind of presence takes a really good friend. It takes a person who trusts that we will eventually "come in out of the rain" and assures us by his or her confidence that he or she will be there when we are able to give of ourselves again.

Be angry but do not sin;

do not let the sun go down on your anger.

EPHESIANS 4:26

3

Anger

A third dimension of the experience of loss and growth is the emotion of anger. Anger is, among other things, the response the body feels when it senses a threat. When we lose someone or something that has helped us know a significant portion of who we are, we feel threatened, which can lead to anger.

When Tom retired, he was surprised by how much anger and rage he felt. He had been looking forward to his retirement as a time to do all the things he had not had time for. But a few weeks after he stopped going to work, he found himself feeling angry and disquieted. Tom had spent forty years of his life as a science teacher and coach at the local high school. When that ended, his self-understanding was threatened. He did not realize how much his sense of worth was tied up in the portion of his identity defined by teaching and coaching.

One way to imagine Tom's reaction and the impact of his loss on his self-understanding is with overlapping roles (see Illustration 1). Tom is the large circle in the middle of the picture. One oval is his role as Malinda's father. Another oval is as Jack's father. Another oval is as Carolyn's husband. Another oval represents his shared life with his father. Another, his life with his mother. Another, his life as a teacher.

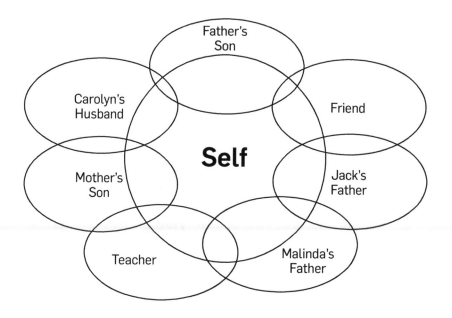

ILLUSTRATION I: SENSE OF SELF

When Tom retired, a large chunk of his self-understanding was torn away (see Illustration 2)—not simply his self-understanding as a teacher. That self-understanding had an impact on the way he related to the other people in his life. Tom's sense of confidence in his own identity was confused. His identity was threatened.

Confusion about our identity often feels like a threat. Anger is the body's production of adrenaline, which enables the animal in us to fight or flee whatever is threatening us. Anger is raw energy that needs to go somewhere. Anger is an honest emotion that must be accepted and addressed or it will go underground in the soul and eat away at our life and vitality.

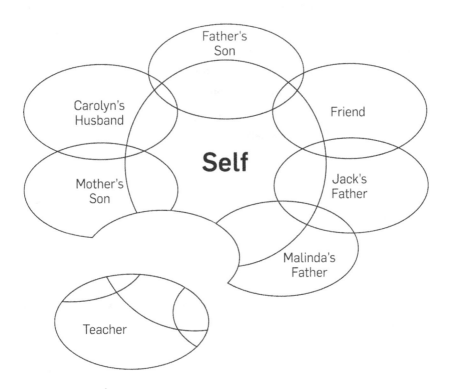

ILLUSTRATION 2: IDENTITY CONFUSION

It helps to notice that the focus of our anger may vary. Sometimes we channel it outward. When Barbara and Jim lost their six-month-old baby to SIDS, among the many things they felt amid the devastation were rage and anger. They were angry at the medical community for not being able to prevent such a tragedy. They were angry at other people whose children were still alive. They were angry at the world for not slowing down and taking into account their pain. They were angry at God for allowing such a sweet child to die. They were angry at the faith community for its powerlessness in the face of such loss.

Sometimes when we lose our innocence, we become angry at the world as well. Several years ago I was on a trip to Cambodia, one of the poorest countries in the world, which had suffered the massive genocide of Pol Pot. I was overwhelmed by the stories of death and destruction and moved to tears by little children who did not have food.

When I returned to my own country with its great wealth, I was angry. I was angry at advertisers for manipulating our greed. I was angry at our government for not caring enough for the rest of the world. I was angry at multinational corporations that only served their own best interests and cared nothing for the foreign workers who made their success possible. When my eyes were opened to the reality of the world I had only seen on television, my vision of myself and my nation as both good and caring was challenged, and I was angry at the world over my loss of innocence.

Anger at loss might also be focused inward. Mike was close to his mother and had never really left home, even though he was forty-two years old. He and his mother got along well except for the times she challenged him about finding a place of his own.

One night while Mike was out with friends his mother had a heart attack. When he came home, he found her on the couch, dead.

Mike experienced not only sadness and fear but also anger. He was angry because he was not there when his mother needed him. He was angry at his mother. But he was angrier at himself, for he felt he had brought on the attack by not getting a place of his own. Mike channeled his anger toward himself. He became depressed and was hospitalized.

To be angry is a natural response to loss. Blaming ourselves because we're angry, however, does no good. Feeling our anger, naming it, and expressing it in ways that don't abuse ourselves or others helps us release it.

To know and feel our anger can help us focus and use that anger in constructive ways. Anger is energy that can help us build a new identity. Focusing our anger on what we can do to live a new life gets us away from being a victim and the desire for someone else to save us from our fears. We can explore what makes us feel strong and what helps us form a new identity independent of what is lost.

It is worth noting that anger is not the only emotion we need to be mindful of when our identity is threatened. Fear can feed our anger. Terror and fear are often present when we have had a significant loss. Because we are unclear about ourselves, we are unclear about what we are capable of. If we don't know what our capacities are, we worry we won't have what is needed to make it in life.

Andrea was terrified. She had trusted Bill to be faithful to his word. She had believed their marriage was solid. When Bill told her he had a brief affair, Andrea was furious. Her anger was fed not only by her sense of betrayal but also because of the loss of trust. She didn't know what to trust any more. She had somehow believed that the future would look something like the past, and she would be sharing life with Bill. Now she didn't know. She feared that the home and the life she had built with Bill would crumble. She was afraid she could not support herself and her children. She was afraid her children would grow up in a home unlike the home she had always dreamed of. Her fear intensified her anger and made it difficult for her to imagine a way to build a future.

When our identity is threatened, we may also experience anxiety. Anxiety comes from a word that means "to choke." When we feel frightened and unclear about who we are, we can become anxious. When our inner strength grows, and we discover we don't need what has been lost to be a self we like and feel good about, we become less anxious. When our anxiety is lessened, we are able to see more options for our future and thus are likely to make better decisions.

I experienced the threat to my identity when I became a professor. Even though I had taught most of my life as a pastor, my image of a professor differed from my image of a teaching pastor. Therefore I was deeply anxious the first couple of years I taught in the seminary. I didn't know the extent of my capacities. I had unrealistic expectations and had to discover what "realistic" might be. I even had troubling dreams at night, adding to my difficulty in dealing with my fear.

As we struggle to grow and change and deal with the losses that accompany those changes, allowing ourselves to feel the anger that rises up is important. It is equally important to express that anger in ways that are consistent with the truth of what is causing it. For example, we should not strike out at our children or at someone when we are feeling threatened by an unrelated issue, such as a possible job loss.

Being in touch with our anger and fear and anxiety is a vital part of growing spiritually. To grow spiritually requires centering our lives in that which can sustain us in the midst of the changing world around us. Spiritual strength is the ability to stay on course even when the winds of threat and fear would knock us off. If we are in touch with our fears and our anger, then we are more aware of what we are putting our trust in. To trust our souls to those things that can be taken from us is to be vulnerable to manipulation by the powers that would control us. To trust in the energy of life that creates and re-creates us, ever calling us into a new world, is to be defined by that which has eternal qualities.

When you are processing loss or growing spiritually, you will feel anger. Let this be and let it teach you. Live the anger and fear and anxiety. It isn't easy. But know it is normal. There is nothing wrong with you. It is a dimension of the experience of learning to live again.

Good Companions

A good companion through this experience of growth and grief is someone not afraid of passion and fire. Anger is scary. It is full of energy and chaos. It often feels as if you are spinning out of control. A good companion is someone not blown over by intense emotions.

Someone who doesn't take attacks personally is helpful. She knows no one can fill all your needs for security and safety. She knows you may strike out against her, but it really isn't about her. She knows you are just scared and don't know whom else to scream at.

A good friend is also one who can help you name what you fear. You may not even know what frightens you. When Deborah and I were on our honeymoon in Saint John, we went snorkeling in the Caribbean. As we floated around looking at the underwater life, I kept breathing in water in my mask. It was frustrating. It spoiled the beauty and the fun. Finally Deborah asked me, "Are you afraid?" I immediately replied, "No, I'm not afraid. What would I be afraid of? I know how to swim."

But as I kept trying to relax and breathe easily, I realized that I was afraid. I had not spent much time in the ocean. I sheepishly confessed to Deborah, and she said, "Let me hold your hand."

I did. Just a few moments of her calming presence released me from my fear, and I could move away from her hand and snorkel on my own. Good companions are ones who can feel and help you name your passions, your fears, and then be present to ease the fears until you can swim on your own.

It is also good to have musical companions. Poetry and music provide ways of expressing that which is too deep for expression. Passionate music and artistic expression that articulates anger and fear, terror and agony, can be helpful during our angry times. We need people around us who can help us find ways to express these deep physical emotions so we can share our feelings. The visual arts also provide healing perspectives. I have a friend who has photographs of tornadoes as his computer screen saver. He says they remind him of the turmoil of his soul and its potentially destructive power. Paintings and photographs that open us to our own fear and chaos help us stay in touch with who we are and what we are experiencing.

Having people around us who can hear the self-doubt that drives much of our anger can also be beneficial. It can be shattering to realize you don't have the power to keep loss from happening and that many times you have no power to restore what was lost. We need individuals who can hold on to our confidence for us even when we doubt everything about ourselves.

Then he took a loaf of bread,

and when he had given thanks,

he broke it and gave it to them, saying,

"This is my body, which is given for you.

Do this in remembrance of me."

LUKE 22:19

4

Remembering

A fourth part of the growing-through-grieving process is remembering. To learn to live again entails spending time remembering what has been lost. We have all retold our stories of loss. Sometimes we think we must be boring other people because we can't seem to stop telling our stories. We tell anyone who will listen—stranger or friend—as we try to come to terms with the absence of someone important to us. Remembering is such a continuous process because significant losses are a loss to the whole self. They affect the mind, heart, body, and soul. The mind, for example, becomes disoriented. We orient ourselves in relationship to significant people and situations.

The space we live in orients us. When people lose a home to flood or fire, their minds become disoriented. Regaining a sense of comfort and space becomes difficult. When we are not in familiar spaces, our minds must work overtime to know where we are and where we might be going. Part of the reason we keep talking about our houses and the way they used to be is to help us reorganize our minds.

Loss has a debilitating effect on the heart as well. The heart is where the affective part of our relationships is carried, the part of us that bonds to the other. When we are bonded, we are a part of their life and they are a part of ours. When we lose a loved one, the heart is stripped of some of its way of knowing itself. To remember, to "re-member" the other person, is the heart's way of reorganizing the shattered and scattered pieces of our life.

Losing someone significant involves a loss to the body as well. Loss is a physical experience. The body has ways of knowing that seem to ignore the mind and heart. In the early years after my first wife died, I found myself becoming distressed in the springtime (near the anniversary of her death). My body would become restless and unsettled. It took a couple of years to realize that my body was remembering my wife's death long before my mind or heart remembered. In some way, deep within the bone marrow, the body has ways of holding the pain of loss that do not require the heart or mind to participate. When we spend time telling the story of the loss, we are trying to cause the body to come to terms with the loss.

Loss reaches deep in the soul too. When our child dies, our soul is stripped of much of the comfort and security it had constructed for itself. The soul may have had a fundamental trust of the universe or God, but when a child is taken from us, the soul must fundamentally reorient itself. The world will never be as friendly as it was before. Underlying the hope for a beneficent world is the truth that the threat of death and chaos lurks at the edges of our fragile hope. To remember, to tell the story over and over, is the soul's way of trying to re-understand and know itself in relation to the forces that hold life and threaten life.

It could be said that through remembering we come to "full body" knowing. When we tell of the one we have lost, we are integrating our body, mind, heart, and soul so that all of who we are fully experiences the truth of the loss.

Telling the story frequently is important because your partner in memory is not there with you. When people who remember with you are not around, you lose a sense of history. Shared history imparts a sense of continuity and intimacy. When you are no longer with a person who shares your history, remembering helps keep that intimacy alive. The memories will never re-create the presence, but memories will still provide foundations on which to build your future.

Remembering, however, entails more than the integrative process. It is a way of slowing down and finding rest in the familiar. Adapting to change and processing the loss that accompanies it is physically, emotionally, spiritually, and intellectually exhausting. To spend time remembering the reality that has been lost opens up a way of resting and allowing your energy to be replenished. Remembering is also a way of creating a memorial. Humans create memorials to powerful experiences of passion. Memorials must represent the magnitude of the experience. New York struggles to come up with the right memorial to represent the evil, terror, heroism, and agony of the attack on the Twin Towers on 9/11. We need something to remind us of its size and of the particular losses of each soul in the rubble. To do this, we have to go over the plans many times to find something (inadequate and impotent as it might be) that represents the fullness of the experience.

We must also remember our loss long enough that it becomes human. Many times when we lose someone in divorce, the offended party makes a demon out of the one who violated the marriage. If we lose someone to death, we may make a saint out of the one who died. Neither reality is finally true. Unless we remember long enough to see that those who are lost were human with all the mixture of good and bad that is present in any of us, our future will be distorted. If the one who left in a divorce remains only dark and evil in the memory of the one left, she might be inclined never to love again or to go on a passionate search for the perfect man. If we lose a lover to death and do not remember long enough that the truth about her humanity comes into focus, we may never be able to love another for who they are—complaining because they do not live up to the saint we once loved. This dimension of the growing-through-grieving process proves fundamental to the recognition of life through loss.

Another dimension closely tied to remembering is forgiveness. We will see later that humans offer one another forgiveness in order to free us for our future.

Forgiveness requires some sense of power, and if we see those we have lost as possessing divine power, it will be difficult for us to learn to move beyond their power into our own power. Remembering the whole of what is lost is critical.

Creating a memorial in the mind and heart enables you to take control of your life again. A memorial is a pocket-sized collection of memories that we can take with us, look at and remember when we want to, and then put away. Jane lost her child to a rare illness. Immediately after the loss occurred, little Melody was everywhere Jane looked. Every piece of clothing had her smell. Every room in the house was filled with her presence. Every song Jane heard and every child she saw reminded her of Melody, and the cutting pain in her heart bled repeatedly. Jane obsessed about Melody. She talked to whoever would listen.

One day Jane was talking to a friend and learned of a little boy with the same disease who could not afford treatment. This knowledge created such pain in Jane that she decided to do something about it. She started a fund to help little Bobby get treatment. Out of that fund grew a memorial fund for children who needed help paying for treatment. Jane's energy and Melody's spirit, which were ever present, coalesced into a particular focus. Jane could now focus her memory so that it wasn't in every nook and cranny in the house and in the community. Every time she saw a sick child, she remembered Melody's death, and unbearable pain rose from deep within her and almost overwhelmed her. But she endured that pain, allowed it to exist, and moved with it to ease the pain of other children and parents. Each child she met and helped added another thread to the fabric of the memorial she was creating to honor her little girl.

Sometimes such a memorial provides some sense to the senselessness of tragedy. Some tragedies will never make sense in terms of the heart, but at least the absurdity of the death has the chance of having some meaning. When you have suffered a significant loss and other people can benefit from your experience, there is at least some hope. By focusing the memory and the energy on the future, the life of the past becomes power for growing your world. As a result of this memorial, Jane has been able to expand her world, and her heart has been touched by dozens of parents and children whom she would have never known. The memorial making we undertake shrinks the pervasive absence of the one we have lost. In its place, we create fresh space for new people, new relationships, and new life.

The danger of remembering our loss is becoming stuck. Gauging when we have remembered long enough can be difficult. No one can tell us when to "get over it." The work of remembering involves downsizing the reality so we can carry it within us into the future. We must create a memorial inside our souls so the life of love that was known remains alive in us, but doesn't control our loving in the future.

The communities of faith, of which many are a part, know that this act of remembering is central to the new life they invite others to experience. The Jewish community is constantly reminded to remember the liberating power of God to bring people from slavery to freedom. The Christian community is constantly called to remember the life and death and resurrection of Jesus. Both are called to remember in hopes of full liberation and healing—effects closely related to God's future hope for humanity. Remembering plays a critical part in learning to live in the future amid profound loss. Keep remembering. Don't let others discourage your memories. Let the memories play over your heart and mind, bathing you in the pain and pleasure they bring.

Good Companions

Helpful companions are people who have time. The process of remembering all the consequences of a loss requires slow time, "porch swing" time. It needs the presence of people whose ease with just sitting and chatting is not obsessed with getting things done.

A good friend is one with whom you can rest and be at ease. Some people seem to be ill at ease when you spend time telling your story over and over. They cut you off by saying, "You told me that before." It may be that this friend should be one who has a bad memory so that each time you tell the story, he or she hears it afresh.

Good companions are also people who can help you create a memorial to what is lost. Ann's six-year-old daughter, Grace, died suddenly of a virulent form of strep. When Grace's sixth birthday came around, there was just an empty space where the parties had been. Some of Ann's cousins gathered with her and took her to a tattoo parlor—not a place Ann frequented. After looking at every kind of picture and finding nothing appropriate, Ann's cousin drew a couple of small bells ringing. (Grace's self-proclaimed nickname was "Gracie Belle.") The tattoo artist's needle buzzed, and now whenever Ann looks down at the inside of her ankle, she sees pink bells ringing—a constant memorial to her little girl. Good companions go with you when you need to find ways to remember.

Individuals who do not have some preconceived notion of what moving on for you would look like may be the most helpful companions for this dimension of the growing process. They need to be open to whatever you are remembering, not wondering when you are going to move to a place where you don't need to remember so much. They know that remembering is a way of resting in familiar places and that this exhausting process requires frequent resting places.

If we say that we have no sin,

we deceive ourselves,

and the truth is not in us.

If we confess our sins,

he who is faithful and just will forgive us our sins

and cleanse us from all unrighteousness.

1 JOHN 1:8-9

5

Guilt

A fifth dimension of growing through change and grieving the loss of that which has been significant is the experience of guilt. This may surprise people, especially if you are not particularly religious. Some people believe guilt is the creation of religious people who want to control others. Indeed, guilt has been exploited by religion to keep people under control.

The fact is, in spite of what we might want to think, guilt is real. To be in community, to live within human circles of care, means people take responsibility for living with each other. When we take responsibility for relationships, we give to and receive from one another. If I am part of a family, I have some negotiated responsibility within that family structure. I may be responsible for making some money to support the family. I may be responsible for contributing to the safety of the children. I may be responsible for helping out with the dishes or taking out the garbage. Responsibility is inherent within any community that has stability and purpose.

That being said, guilt is a real dimension of responsible communities. *Guilt* is the term used when one does not fulfill one's task. *Guilt* is the term used when we do not give what we have claimed we will give. Therefore, whenever a significant loss occurs, we begin to raise questions about what we should or should not have done.

I have been with many people as they grieved the loss of a marriage. Most people go into marriage with the expectation that it will last. Most people I know make decisions that they believe will contribute to the well-being and longevity of their relationships. They begin their marriages trying to live in a way that contributes to the happiness of the two people in the marriage.

As any marriage progresses, issues arise that become difficult to process. Frequently arguments and fights may ensue. Two people with independent thoughts will disagree. During the arguments or fights, each will be hurt. Each will wound the other—intentionally or unintentionally. Most of the painful disagreements include not only the sharing of different ideas but also the challenge of ideas that represent what we believe about ourselves. When these arguments cut into our feelings about the character of the other, the pain is deep and the hurt is real. If this situation goes on long enough, some marriages hit the wall and one of the partners may decide to leave the relationship. Most people who are honest about their divorces will say there were plenty of factors in the relationship that contributed to the demise of the marriage. Most people would also say there was enough blame to go around. After the painful departure, when each person is trying to defend herself or himself against the accusations of the other, each can think of things done during the marriage that might have been done differently. Frequently they feel guilty about not having done those things that might have saved their marriage.

Now this kind of guilt isn't simply limited to two adults in a relationship. Guilt is sometimes visited on anyone who believes she or he had power to make a difference but didn't. Michael was thirteen when his parents divorced. His own turmoil as an early adolescent combined with the tension in the marriage between his parents. When they finally separated, Michael experienced much guilt. He felt as if his angry outbursts and his resistance to his parents' requests had been responsible for his parents splitting up.

Guilt isn't just limited to relationships for which we have responsibility or had the power to act. Guilt also may be present even when there was nothing we could have done. Gary is weighted with a guilt he can hardly stand. His daughter had just turned sixteen and had her license. She wanted to borrow the family car and visit a friend. Gary agreed and gave her the keys. Just a mile from their home, the car was struck broadside by a car that ran a red light and his daughter was killed.

Mixed in with all Gary's pain and aching agony of losing his daughter was a sense of guilt. This would not have happened had he just said no. Maybe he had not been a good enough teacher and taught his daughter about defensive driving. If he had just bought the new car he had been putting off, the side air bags would have saved her life. Guilt rides the vehicles of "what if" and "if only," driving us to near insanity. Merely telling Gary he is not responsible will not suffice. He feels responsible, and guilt will be his constant companion.

Many people believe that this kind of guilt is closer to a primal shame. Some therapists believe that when an infant is born, she has a sense that she is the center of the universe. She believes she possesses the ability to make people around her do what she wants done. But early on, that sense of certainty is replaced by a growing sense that she can't make the events that affect her happen. She comes to know that she does not have power to control her world. She feels inadequate. Some would say this sense of inadequacy produces shame. We feel we are not worthy because we don't have the power to make things happen that we think would be good for us.

These feelings of inadequacy and powerlessness and shame are the reasons that we must spend time dealing with guilt in the grieving process. Sorting out what we are really responsible for and what we have no power to control is vital. If we can honestly assess our responsibility and what we really have the power to change, then we can open ourselves to forgiveness. We can understand that we made certain mistakes without carrying around the burden of believing we could have changed everything.

Processing is important even if you can't think your way out of your dilemma. Processing enables you to sort out what power you actually have. Sometimes our sense of guilt is related to our belief that we have godly power. Molly was a religious woman, and she went to church regularly. When her husband got sick with cancer, Molly prayed for his healing. Her community prayed as well. Earnest petitions were sent up to God on behalf of her husband, but he did not survive.

One part of Molly's mind knew that she could not have saved her husband. Another part would not give up the idea that she had not prayed hard enough. At some level Molly believed that her prayers had gone unanswered because she was not good enough. If she been a better person, would God have answered her prayer? Guilt rested squarely inside Molly's soul.

Understanding guilt and processing not only what was our responsibility but also what we controlled helps us move beyond the painful losses of our lives. Exploring our feelings will help us give up our need and desire to be divine. It will help us realize that we are human and that we can give only what we have. Admitting our responsibility for a broken relationship is an important part of opening up to forgiveness.

Naming our limits and accepting our humanity also opens us up to the delightful human future beyond our pain. When we realize our limits, we are not tempted to overfunction in the future. If we believe we have omnipotent power, we will always worry we are not doing enough to make things work out better. We will be tempted to believe that everything is about us and that we must do everything right to ensure nothing goes wrong. However, when we remember that we can only influence certain things and that many events are beyond our control, then we can do well with what is our responsibility and not carry unreal expectations for ourselves. Many people miss the sheer delight of living because they take on more responsibility than is theirs to take.

When we are realistic about our responsibility, then we can also be realistic about our mistakes. We can work on things that can be corrected.

The PBS documentary *What I Want My Words to Do to You* tells the story of Eve Ensler, who spends several months working with inmates in a maximum-security prison for women. She guides them in a writing workshop that helps the women sort out which aspects of their situation resulted from their choices and which aspects resulted from being victimized. In working this out, the inmates begin to realize that they are more than the mistakes they have made. Ensler teaches the prison population that society creates prisons as monuments to the mistakes people have made and that, before she worked with these women, she also had seen them as mistakes. They had become their mistakes. But now, after she had worked with them, Ensler saw them as women who had made mistakes.

Ensler's realization illustrates the growth that can occur if we admit our guilty feelings when facing a loss. If we stay with our feelings and explore the truth about our responsibilities and our limits, we cannot become a mistake. Instead, we can see ourselves as persons who make mistakes and who are therefore capable of forgiveness, which frees us from the power of those mistakes so we can come alive in a new future.

Good Companions

The people who walk well with you as you experience your guilt are the people who know guilt in their own lives. They are people who know they have made mistakes and understand that you feel you have made them too. You do not need someone to talk you out of your feelings. It can't be done. To try to do so is just irritating. You need someone to affirm your feelings of guilt.

You also need to be around individuals who have experienced grace. We all have been loved when we don't deserve it. When we are feeling pain and not liking ourselves, we need people around who know what it is like to have received love when they didn't feel worthy of it. This kind of person is one who stays present and is not pushed away by your "bitchiness" or your selfishness. They love you even when you don't know yourself as lovable.

It is good if this person can ask thoughtful questions, for it helps you to sort through which situations you have responsibility for and which are beyond your capacity to change. Admitting you don't have the power to make situations right or to bring back someone who has gone may not be easy, but by thinking about it over and over, you eventually come to accept what is yours and what is not yours.

If you are a religious person, walking awhile with a person of faith, who can assure you that your community trusts in forgiveness, is helpful. Priests, pastors, and rabbis have the responsibility to tell the stories of faith that reflect the mercy of God for creatures. Some will help you find ways to open yourself to that forgiving mercy by offering activities that offset the mistakes you might have made. Others will assure you that the community of which you are a part and the God you worship loves you and will support you even if you feel guilty.

If you are a person of faith, rereading stories of your ancestors in faith, in which mercy and grace were made evident, can also be beneficial. Jews, Muslims, and Christians all share common stories of God's mercy. The story of Cain and Abel reveals a God whose mercy extends to one who has killed his brother. While God exacts some penalty on Cain for his crime, God also offers Cain an opportunity to live life, to create family, and to have a future. This and many other stories told within the faith community help us realize that guilt is real and that forgiveness is possible. Knowing this opens us to receiving forgiving grace for our future.

And just then some people were

carrying a paralyzed man lying on a bed.

When Jesus saw their faith,

he said to the paralytic,

"Take heart, son;

your sins are forgiven."

MATTHEW 9:2

6

Forgiving

The way to new life, or the way to living without the presence of someone or something that has been significant, requires that a person live through several dimensions of life.

- Naming the losses that have happened or that will happen helps you to grow and move beyond where you are.
- Feeling the pain of the loss helps you know more deeply the truth of the loss.
- Getting in touch with the anger that resides in the loss helps you discover energy for new life.
- Remembering what is lost helps free you from a free-floating memory and focuses that memory so you can move into the future.
- Identifying the guilt you feel because of what you did or did not do to contribute to the loss, or the guilt you feel over not having power to stave off the loss, helps you discover the limits of your own humanness.

When we have experienced these things, sometimes we are visited with the gift of a forgiving spirit. Once we have struggled and identified the experiences of our humanity and the humanity of others, we may find ourselves being more gracious toward others or ourselves. A forgiving spirit comes to us as a gift when we are no longer dependent on what we have lost for our sense of well-being.

It is important to realize that forgiveness does not mean we are free from the memory of the past. We don't forgive and forget. The past remains an integral part of who we are. The pain of our loss becomes central to our new self-understanding. Remembering the pain protects us from entering into situations that are dangerous for us.

Sally was taught that forgiving and forgetting was a virtue to be cherished. She was in a relationship with a man who abused her. Her marriage bound her not only to her husband as he cherished her but also as he beat her. She believed that her faith required that she forgive him. For Sally, forgiving included forgetting the abuse for which she forgave him. Because she bound forgiveness with forgetting, she continued to expose herself to a life that diminished her.

To forgive but not forget allows the memory of the loss to shape what we do with our future but not to control what we do. To remember danger keeps us from putting ourselves in dangerous situations in the future. To forgive another person who has harmed us does not require that we subject ourselves to the dangers again but may mean we move on with our lives without that person's presence in our home.

Knowing the pain we have been through also creates in us a compassionate spirit for others who are in pain. We do not want to forget the loss or that which has disappeared because it was a part of the life we value, a part of the cadre of people who made up who we have become. What we have lost is a part of what has made us the interesting person we are.

Forgiveness is not freedom from the memory of the past. True forgiveness entails freedom from being controlled by what happened in the past. Whether our loss is by choice (I decided to leave her) or by circumstance (he died), anger and guilt will be a part of the loss. The power of that anger and guilt to control our future will lessen if we allow the forgiving spirit to be part of our lives. Forgiving isn't an easy thing to do. We want to be responsible people, and we want others to be responsible. It may feel as if we are excusing others' actions if we allow forgiveness to become part of the fabric of our soul. But by remembering what happened, forgiveness does not excuse. It remembers the pain; it remembers the person and his or her limits and humanity, and it does not allow that memory to define how we will interact with that person in the future.

Forgiveness reminds us that the past was not all we needed it to be—and probably could not have been. Mark had to forgive his father, who had not protected him from the pressures of a chaotic life. Mark's father had an addiction that resulted in his inability to support his son consistently. When his father died, Mark struggled. His anger over his father's death was compounded by his anger over his father's addiction. Only when Mark was able to remember his dad with all his gifts and graces, along with his pain and inadequacies, was he able to forgive him. Forgiving didn't mean that Mark excused his father's behavior. It simply meant Mark didn't allow the pain to distort the full truth about his father.

When Mark was able to forgive his dad, he discovered a new sense of grace in himself toward his own inadequacies. Only when he was freed from the power of his father's mistakes was Mark able to be less afraid of his own mistakes.

Forgiveness frees up energy for a more adventuresome life. You know you are moving past the pain of the loss when you find you are open to new adventures.

Forgiving others in our lives may require exploring our relationship to the divine power in the universe. Being angry at God in a time of loss is not unusual. Anger at God was a common experience for many of the spiritual greats of the past. The ancient scriptures contain multiple examples of songs (like Psalm 44) that express the Jewish people's anger (as individuals and as a nation) at the Holy One for not protecting them or for not punishing their enemies. Their anger was born from the belief that God did not act justly. Jesus expressed what some believe to be anger at God when he felt deserted at his death. Similarly, when we face losses that seem to result from inaction by a divine force who (we believe) could have prevented the loss, we may grow angry. But as we explore those feelings of anger, we may wonder if a forgiving spirit would be valuable. We may never come to the point of forgiveness, but it is possible to prevent the loss of the past to control completely the way one relates to the universe in the future. When a flood or some natural disaster destroys one's home or when a loved one dies in a tragic accident or from cancer, anger at God and the inability to forgive are a natural reaction. But a forgiving spirit remains open to the sunshine and the grace of spring flowers—even while anger exists.

All of these dimensions of processing growth and loss do not always occur sequentially. There may be days when you are angry, immediately followed by days when you have energy for a creative future. Days of deep sadness and tears may be followed by mellow and poignant days of musing and memory. Forgiveness has a way of weaving itself back and forth through the multiple dimensions of the process. As you grow toward the new person you are becoming, you will realize that you have more energy for the future and spend less and less time remembering the pain and struggle of the past. You will find yourself eagerly taking responsibility for a different future and not worrying about what you or others might have done in the past. You will discover that your desire for the future will be accompanied by the strength to make decisions for yourself without trying to name blame for what happened. Forgiveness is not something that comes full blown. It comes a bit at a time. Be open to the gift when it comes. Allow it to mellow your heart and release you from the power of the past to control your future.

Good Companions

Notice the people around you who have gone through significant changes in their lives and who seem to have an energy and vitality for living. Visit them and ask them to tell you about their losses. Ask them to tell you how angry they felt and then how they were freed from the anger. They may never have talked about it, but when you are around these people, you know they have somehow moved beyond the pain to new discoveries and excitement.

Other people who may be helpful to you in these times are those who can mirror back to you your own humanity in a loving way. That is, good friends are people who can help you find humor in your own humanness. They can gently help you see that your moral indignation against another or against the loss may be a little over the top and that you too share some of the same characteristics of those you judge. When we see in ourselves what we hate in another, we are more open to grace. We can at least see that our future does not depend on remaining attached to the other through our anger at them.

Good friends are also people who can live with us in a way that pulls our past out of us and awakens us to the possibility of a vital future. People who excite our life energy help us realize that the past is just that—past. They help us realize there is life to be lived in the future. Their presence captures our delight and helps us taste the future. Our taste of the future might tease our hunger for something new, the way the aroma of freshly baked bread draws us to the kitchen.

*O come, let us sing to the L*ORD*;*

   let us make a joyful noise to the rock of our salvation!

Let us come into his presence with thanksgiving;

   let us make a joyful noise to him with songs of praise!

PSALM 95:1-2

7

Gratitude

When you (or someone you know) have struggled through the pain and anger of a loss and have allowed the forgiving spirit to begin to do its work, then you begin to discover the seventh dimension of the process: gratitude. Early in any loss, the intensity of your pain can be so profound that you are unable to see the whole picture. You often look at the past through the lens of pain and fear. Your memory of the person you have lost may be colored by the most intense and most recent experiences. But that memory is not the whole picture. There were other times when a larger, more complete picture existed.

You will know that forgiveness of yourself and others has begun when you can look at the past and find gifts for which you are grateful. Some of what you see will be fairly obvious, making it easy to be grateful. When you lose your job at retirement, you can look back on that job and be grateful for the bread and butter it put on your plate and the roof it put over your head. Even if the job was not the most satisfying work, it provided the necessities of life. You can also be grateful for some of the people you knew because they shared your work with you. You may feel grateful that there was some structure to your life and that you didn't have to make decisions every day about what you were going to do.

Other losses may reveal other gifts that are not so obvious. One of the gifts that came to me when my first wife died was new eyes with which to see my adult children. I had raised my children, but even though they were young adults I still treated them as children. I tried to protect them from the hard things of life—hoping they would not be hurt. I didn't realize what I was doing until I was unable to do it any more. I was so distressed over my losses that I didn't have the energy to protect my children or to try to take care of them.

I distinctly remember the day I called each of them and told them I now needed their help. I needed them in some way I was not yet able to articulate. When I admitted my own need and realized I could not protect them from the pain I was feeling, I learned what gifted adults they were. They stepped forward and were able to stand by me in my pain, helping me discern truth in my own experience. Because of our loss, we discovered new strength in each other that has served us well in moving toward our own future.

To recognize gratitude in the midst of loss does not diminish the value of what is lost. It simply admits that there are doors of discovery that open when other doors are closed. Rose found herself alone after thirty-five years of marriage. Her husband had died after a long illness. After much struggle, she realized she had been so dependent on her husband that she had lost her own identity. She had been known primarily as "Harry's wife," which was how she had known herself as well. Life was difficult for her after he died. Rose had to learn how to do many things Harry had always done. She had to find a way to support herself. She had to initiate relationships with friends.

As she moved through the dimensions of growth and grief, Rose was able to name many of the gifts she had received in Harry's dying. She realized she was a strong woman who could stand by someone in the darkest hour. She realized she was a good partner and that the two of them had had many rich and joyful experiences in their life. Even as she worked through her anger and fear at Harry's dying, Rose's memories filled her with moments of laughter and love. She was able to discern gifts beyond what she had known with Harry. She could give thanks for the freedom that was now hers. She could choose to come and go as she pleased. She could travel and explore new places. She could spend the whole weekend in her pajamas. She could try new restaurants without worrying about Harry. For Rose, admitting that she enjoyed these things was not easy. In many ways it felt as if she were happy Harry had died. But soon she realized that she was simply celebrating the new life she had been given.

The ability to move into the dimension of gratitude plays a critical part of the healing process. Gratitude becomes an important component in our ability to grow spiritually. For to grow is to embrace the reality of our lives for what they have become, and not simply to lament because they are no longer something we have lost. Everyone loses. Some find joy in the new life they enter into, while others live in the fear that allowing themselves to live and love again will expose them to pain again.

One of the greatest gifts of my life as a pastor was to know people over long periods of time and to discover how they lived their lives. Many of the people with whom I worked were over sixty-five and had experienced several significant losses. Their world had changed, and their own personal tragedies had piled up.

Some of the people with whom I ministered seemed sad and embittered, angry that life was no longer the way it had been. They were disappointed that their new life wasn't all they had hoped it would be. Whenever change was a possibility in the church, they responded with resistance and sometimes anger. I had the feeling that another significant loss would push them over the edge. It might even push them into deeper bitterness.

Other people who had experienced a similar series of changes and losses in their lives seemed interested in exploring new things. They looked back on their lives and were grateful for what had been, but they allowed that perspective to free them to consider the future as a place for new gifts as well. I am not sure what the difference between these people was, but it seems as if the members of the former group had never grieved their losses.

The pain of that which they had lost seemed to be stuck in their souls and caused them to fear any further change. The members of the latter group remembered their past, were grateful for the gifts it had given to them, and were thus open to the gifts that the future might offer as well. Remember the gifts of pleasure and pain. Each has within it possibilities for a new future. Each has resources for living that will be helpful as you open your heart to the new life emerging within you and around you.

Good Companions

People who seem to know genuine joy are good companions to help you notice and explore gratitude as a dimension of growth through loss. These are not the people who seem to be perpetually happy and thus oblivious to the fullness of life. These are people who know the struggle but who have sifted through the rubble of their own lives and found gifts under the garbage. These people feel both pain and pleasure deeply and know that all life is a bit of both.

Good friends are also individuals who will welcome your new discoveries with as much delight as you do. When we have wandered around in the wilderness of despair and darkness, some of what we discover as gifts may not shine very brightly to others who have not been where we are. But they are important to us. A good friend is one who finds those gifts to be just as amazing as you do.

After I left congregational ministry and started teaching, I lived in constant amazement at the freedom my new career gave me. I had lived under the perpetual demand to preach each week, to declare myself on a topic that seemed important to me and to others. At times the pressure became overwhelming. And although I missed the ritual of preaching as an organizing discipline when I left the ministry, being free from the pressure and time constraints of preaching was also a gift.

As a pastor, I had also lived with a to-do list that was never completed. I went to bed every night with a long list of people to see and books to read and sermons to write. Even when I took a day off to relax and catch my breath, the to-do list hung around in the back of my mind, weighing down my spirit as I sought to play. When I became a professor, I discovered that although there were periods of intense work during the school year, I had my summers off. A whole summer to travel and explore the world! I also had breaks between semesters. Students came into class for fourteen weeks, then there was a break and we had new students. I was amazed at the possibility of having a life less structured by the demands of my job. I shared the delight with my new friends who had been living this life. It seemed normal to them. They patiently listened to me as I went on about the joy of this freedom.

As you journey through your pilgrimage of loss, find people who can share your delight. When you speak your gratitude, it becomes more real. Gratitude shared has a longer life.

Find persons to write to—even if to yourself. Either through letters or journals, find ways of writing about your gifts. Express the delight and joy in the life you shared with the one you lost, as well as the discoveries you are making about yourself and the world now that you no longer have that relationship. Both the memories and the new discoveries are gifts for which one can be thankful. When you write them down, they become more visible, and when you share them, others can remind you of their presence in those times when you might forget. When you write them in a journal, you can return to them when clouds descend in your soul and you feel nothing is worth living for. These discoveries will feed you when you are hungry for hope.

"The wind blows where it chooses,

and you hear the sound of it,

but you do not know where it comes from

or where it goes."

JOHN 3:8

8

Play

To learn to live again as a new person after you have lost important parts of who you are requires the ability to play again. You will know you are moving more into the world of the new self when you find yourself playing with new ways of doing things. To play is to live out a new way of life within the safety of uncommitted space.

When children play, they grow and become new and different people. When my son was three years old, he would go in my closet and pull down a shirt and tie. He would put the shirt on with the tail dragging the floor. He would tie a knot in the tie and put it around his neck. He put on my sneakers and stumbled around the house pretending to be grown up. He was trying on what it felt like to be a man. He was able to pretend without the responsibility, which is the way children grow into new and different ways of being in the world. They look at adults and then pretend to cook in the kitchen or to teach in the classroom.

When we have had a significant loss, we do not lose only our partner, our home, our job, or our child. We also lose our identity. We mourn the loss not only of the other but also of ourselves in relation to the other. To become something other than what we have been requires that we try on new clothes.

When a student graduates from college, she often becomes uncertain of her identity. She has earned a degree, but what will she do with it? It is not at all unusual for someone in that situation to "try on" several jobs. These jobs are ways of playing with who she sees herself becoming. If she is single and does not have responsibility for family or friends, she has the freedom to try different jobs. Knowing who we are becoming is hard unless we have a chance to try on different identities.

If we have been married and find ourselves single again, dating can be one way to visualize who we are becoming. It allows us to feel and see what lives within us. Dating serves as a way of finding what we want to be and also finding someone whom we can love. And since whom we love shapes who we become, the presence of the other person helps us know what we want to be. We grow to love not only the other person but also what we become when we are with them. We play our way into new ways of being and living. Dating different people helps us uncover different dimensions of ourselves and therefore imagine becoming a new person.

To grow spiritually involves imagining ourselves as different kinds of people, playing with different ways of being in the world. I have come to imagine this growth by seeing the self as composed of four quadrants. We know ourselves by the voices we listen to from within each of those quadrants. Imagine a large X (see Illustration 3). In the quadrant on the left are the voices from our past—the voices of parents and teachers, family and mentors, anyone who has helped shape our values. The voices in the top quadrant speak to us from the contemporary world: the voices of news, advertisement, music, our children, our boss, and others with whom we live, whose presence shapes what we do with our time. The voices in the bottom quadrant are voices of the soul, the whispering voices of conscience, intuition, and emotion. The voices in this quadrant reflect our unique way of responding to our world and what we most value and fear. The voices in the quadrant on the right are voices of the future. These voices combine the imagination and the offers that the future extends to us. They whisper and seduce us toward them, giving us activities to live for tomorrow.

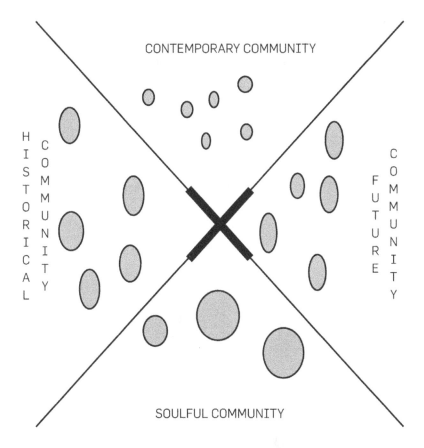

CONTEMPORARY COMMUNITY

SOULFUL COMMUNITY

ILLUSTRATION 3

Most of us live our lives by paying attention to the voices closest to the center of the X (see Illustration 4). We listen to voices that create a balanced circle that reinforces what we know ourselves to be. We try to create equilibrium by listening to the voices that create the most peace for us. For example, if we are married and have a family, we listen to voices from our past that tell us that we are to be responsible and faithful to this family. We then listen to people within the contemporary world of voices who help us do that. We listen to our soul's values that nurture that activity. And we plan activities that will serve our goal of being responsible and faithful to our family. We generally try to quiet the voices in the four quadrants that would seduce us into being unfaithful to those responsibilities. Our lives have some balance and we can function to produce the desired effect.

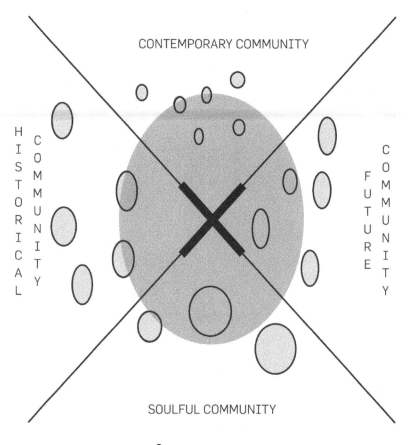

ILLUSTRATION 4

When a crisis occurs, the balanced circle in the center of the X spins out of control and creates an imbalance. A crisis can be like a balloon filled with air. If you let it go and the air comes out, the balloon flies crazy-like, here and there. It creates chaos. It won't follow a straight line but performs a scattering, spinning dance in the sky (see Illustration 5).

For example, if you lose your job, everything in the circle is threatened. Your ability to be responsible, as you know responsibility, is threatened. The voices of your boss and the people at work are no longer the dominant voices in the contemporary world. Suddenly you are listening to other voices in the quadrant—voices that might offer another way of being responsible. The voices of your soul that speak to you of your self-doubt—voices that might have been silenced as you were functioning capably in your previous job—begin to cry out, and anxiety sets in. Suddenly the voices from your future that invite you to consider a new career begin to sound more interesting.

Growth occurs when someone begins to pay attention to voices outside the comfortable circle of balance and equilibrium. When we begin to play with other ways of living our lives, we create the opportunity for growth.

This process isn't simply the way we create growth when there has been a loss but is the way we grow in all our life. To be alive is to need stability and adventure, predictability and surprise. We need to pay attention to the familiar and ordered voices of our familiar communities. We need to know that we belong and to feel the safety of routine and ritual. But if we really are alive, we also need the adventure generated by strange voices.

We need the challenge of being around the exotic and unusual voices of strangers who live life in very different ways. If we live only with the comfortable and familiar, we can become lethargic and dull. If we live only with the strange and adventuresome, we will feel chaotic and disordered. To be a growing and living creature, we rest with the familiar voices and play with the strange ones. That balance can contribute to a life that is not only stable but also adventuresome.

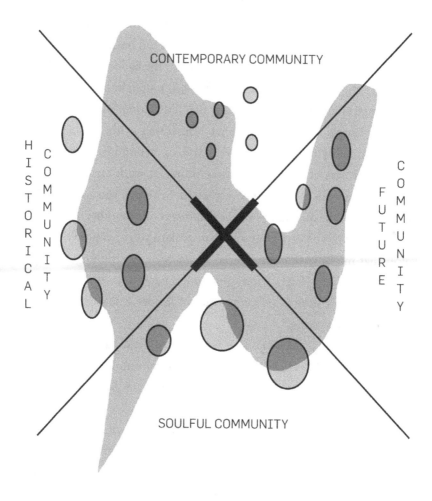

CONTEMPORARY COMMUNITY

HISTORICAL

COMMUNITY

FUTURE

COMMUNITY

SOULFUL COMMUNITY

ILLUSTRATION 5

It is important to remember that play requires grace. When we play, we make mistakes. When we feel uncertain about who we are and our own strengths and weaknesses, we will make mistakes. We will, in many ways feel like little children.

Ron had worked hard and was lucky. He had accumulated enough material wealth to retire at fifty-three. He was excited. No longer did he have to punch a time clock. He didn't have to be accountable to the company. He was free. When he retired, however, he reported he felt scared in his newfound freedom, like a child learning to walk. He would try to figure out what to do with his day and be unsure about his choices. Forgiveness and grace are vital ingredients when one is in new and unfamiliar territory. In order to become new and different people, we must have the freedom to make mistakes without becoming our mistakes.

You will know that you are moving toward becoming a new person when the spirit of play returns to your life. You may even realize you don't want play to be absent in your new life. You may want to open up to a life of spiritual growth and discovery, expanding your world of memory, of presence, of soul, and of the future by making decisions to risk losing old ways of being to explore new ways of living.

Good Companions

Good companions for this dimension of your experience are people who do not depend on your listening to only those voices in the safe circle. Good companions are people who allow you to try on new clothes without judging you as silly or who do not laugh at you for trying to dance if you don't know how. You need people around you who can accept the idea that you may change your mind about what you value and how you want to spend your time. You need people who can listen to you as you imagine how you will be different in the future.

One of the best friends I had during my time of discovery is the person who became my wife. Deborah and I were experiencing many of the same feelings, living in the chaos of trying to figure out who we were going to be since the worlds we had lived in collapsed around us. We didn't need the other person to be something for us because we didn't know what that other person had to offer. As we came to know each other, we realized that neither of us knew the person who had lived in the past. We only knew what we or others had told us about our past.

For example, Deborah didn't know that I had spent thirty years of my life in a suit and tie. She had known me only as someone who wore jeans and sweatshirts. She didn't realize that I had enjoyed a disciplined life of office and home. She knew me only as someone who wandered the planet, following my impulses to travel and explore the world.

When we are playing with new possibilities in becoming new selves, it is a good thing to have individuals around us who can simply delight in who we are now and do not need us to be what we once were.

This, of course, is hard to do. Most of us live in social systems that limit our relationships with strangers. If a couple has been married twenty-five years and their children leave the house, changing the way they relate to each other is difficult. Each individual has become so familiar with the patterned habits of the other that it becomes frightening to consider that the other person might change in some way.

Yet that fresh and new way of being creates excitement and adventure. Many marriages have trouble when the children leave home. The couple does not know how to be with each other in a new way. When this occurs, each spouse needs to have opportunity to explore new friendships and new hobbies that will help them become new. As the individuals in the marriage take on new dimensions, the marriage will have the potential to take on new dimensions.

Another kind of friend who can be helpful in these times is one who comes to you through books. Books are rich with characters who live life in different ways, and these stories can trigger your imagination. In your mind you can play with new possibilities. You can talk about them with people around you. You can play in your mind long before you try things in your life. When you do try something different, it will not be as you imagined, but at least the imagination helps you prepare for what might be different.

You shall put these words of mine in your heart and soul,

and you shall bind them as a sign on your hand,

and fix them as an emblem on your forehead.

Teach them to your children,

talking about them when you are at home and when you

  are away,

when you lie down and when you rise.

Write them on the doorposts of your house and on your

  gates,

so that your days and the days of your children may

be multiplied in the land that the LORD swore to your

ancestors to give them,

as long as the heavens are above the earth.

DEUTERONOMY 11:18-21

9

Practice

A ninth dimension discovered by those who are growing through grieving is that of practice. After we have explored a variety of options for living again, somewhere along the way we will discover that some of those options represent who we are more than others. When we come to that awareness, we begin practicing those options more than others. If you are dating and discover that one man helps you know yourself the way you want to know yourself, then you spend more time with him. If we are exploring different jobs, eventually we come to a point where one job satisfies more than another, and we settle into that job.

I was a pastor for thirty years and served in three congregations during that time. When I was unable to continue in congregational leadership, I was called to be a professor. Resetting my trajectory after thirty years, I had to spend time exploring what it meant. I had to imagine how to be in the seminary. I spent large chunks of time wandering the country in my car, talking with strangers and watching how others lived their lives. Over time it became clear that the role of professor was more satisfying for me than other options.

The first thing to do when we feel ready to become the person we imagine ourselves to be is to choose a course of action. This decision is often difficult because it means sacrificing other options. We are already working through one loss, and by settling on a particular choice we cut ourselves off from other options. If we don't make a decision, however, we cannot commit ourselves to doing those things that bring new life.

Once I made the decision to become a professor, I worked at practicing the art of teaching. I had to cut myself off from the other choices I might have made and only practice teaching. The discipline of practice creates the difference between one who merely plays the piano and one who is an accomplished pianist. Similarly, the discipline of writing makes the difference between writing and being a writer; committing oneself to the art of drawing makes the difference between one who draws and an artist.

At this point in the process of growing through grieving, we allow our love for what we are becoming to shape how we spend our time. When a child is born into a family, members of the family lose the life they had before the child was born. By virtue of the birth, we are called parents. Most of us begin this process stumbling around, wondering if we really are parents and if we can actually be parents. As we commit ourselves to the child we love and as we practice the skills, acting and making mistakes and learning from those mistakes and acting again, we eventually become the role we are playing.

As we spend more time living the role we are learning, we often grow in our love for it. But to fall in love with the idea of a new way of being and actually to love that way of being are two different things. Sarah fell in love with the idea of being a teacher. She was drawn to it because she enjoyed the teachers she'd had as a student. She enjoyed the exploration of ideas and the adventure of discovery.

When Sarah became a teacher, however, the enchantment wore off. She came to understand that what had drawn her to teaching was her experience of being a student. When she learned that teaching required more than simply exploring ideas, she wondered about her choice. She struggled with all the paperwork required by the administration. She lost sleep over the parent/teacher conferences in which parents became defensive for their children. She worked to keep up her energy as she graded papers into the night.

Even so, the more Sarah worked at teaching, the more she became a teacher. She discovered that loving teaching and learning kept her focused on what was required to ensure that the students had a chance to know the excitement of learning that she had known.

When the time comes on the journey of learning to live a new life, you need to make a decision and begin to practice it. Obviously the commitment may lead you to the awareness that you do not really want to pursue that way of being. But until a commitment is made, the full effect of the new direction will not be known. When Deborah and I were first dating, we struggled to determine how committed we wanted to be. We dated, got close, and then were scared off. We did not see each other for several months before we tried it again. When we dated that second time, once again we began to bump up against resistances within ourselves that pushed us apart. Eventually we decided we liked ourselves better together than separated—so we committed to our love. We practiced that love and stayed together through the hard parts, which eventually led us to a marriage commitment. Now, as any of you who have lived in a committed relationship know, how a relationship looks from the outside is different from what actually exists on the inside. Although we committed ourselves to love and cherish each other, the practice of that commitment is what brought about the new life of cherished love.

To grow spiritually requires similar practice. It requires the practice of paying attention—of slowing down and noticing what is going on around you and within you. Many of us are so eager to live that we miss the living going on within us. We are so eager to know more and do more that we miss what is happening right around us. To grow spiritually is to be open to the moving of the creative energy in the life within and around us.

Paying attention requires intentionality. It requires that we get off the interstates and fast trains and travel the scenic routes. Some people find meditation or Centering Prayer helpful in this task. These practices are disciplines that, once you have committed to them, should be done even when you feel there's not enough time or when you don't have the desire to do them. Stop for twenty or thirty minutes and close your eyes, breathing in the air around you. Relax your muscles into the chair and allow yourself to be held. Slow down the chaos of your mind and focus on some scene or word that quiets the anxiety of your soul. Notice your own heartbeat, your own blood coursing through your veins, your own skin as it is teased by your hair. Notice life within you, allowing the barriers of speed and noise to fade away. With this practice, the quiet voices within have a chance to whisper their longings, and you come to know yourself better.

The positive consequence of paying attention to yourself in this manner is that you begin to slow down and notice the world around you as well. You discover a giftedness in simply being, that you don't need more things or more activities, that life is already here as a gift to you. You notice the gifts that had been yours and that are yours now. You remember the moments of change and new life that have come to you in the past.

Another way that you might practice paying attention is by journaling (see "A Discovery Journal," page 123). Take time every day to write the life you notice around yourself and within yourself. Notice the small things. One discipline that helps is to recall the most insignificant thing that happened to you today and then reflect on it. It's easy to think of the important or big things that might have occurred, but when you try to think of the most inconsequential thing that happened, you have to reflect on almost everything. You have to take notice of the life that is yours. What happens is that you discover life in the most unexpected places. Deciding and then practicing the new life you have identified is one of the things that happens on the way to becoming new.

Good Companions

One of the hardest parts of this dimension in your journey toward newness is discovering people who can help you stay focused on your new life.

Most of us are part of social networks that have a stake in our returning to normal; the people we interact with are not interested adapting so we can be different. It requires a strong person with good social support to develop new ways of responding to the world around him or her. One of the most important things you can watch for in your journey toward the future is one or more individuals who can help you practice the new life. This means finding persons who truly hear what you like about who you are becoming and who then hold you accountable to the vision you have for yourself.

Some counselors excel at this. As I was struggling to find a new way and to become more comfortable with the absence of many things that had made me who I was, I encountered a counselor who walked with me. One of his primary contributions was that he remembered who I was from week to week and gently reminded me of it when I went to see him. When we are alone in the world and making our way, we are living in social systems that want us to be what they need us to be. So when someone walks with us and helps us remember who we are becoming, he or she enables us to practice that new way of living. In sports, coaches are responsible for holding players accountable to the disciplines that help them become the kind of player they want to be. It is often easy to give in to old patterns that are not effective at improving one's skills, and a good coach helps a player stay focused on the best disciplines for better results.

There are business and life coaches whose purpose is the same thing. They listen carefully to us and help us to understand exactly what we are becoming. They then visit with us with some regularity, asking us questions to keep us focused on what we said we wanted to become. They help us consider and establish disciplines that we believe will produce the kind of person we want to be, and then they remind us of those disciplines each time we visit with them. Coaches and counselors can be invaluable in our effort to grow the new dimensions that are emerging within us.

Other companions who help us in this task of practicing the new self are people who have had some success in becoming more effective in being who they desire to be. I have discovered writers who are effective in communicating the way I want to. I have visited with them and read books by them on what they do to make it possible to produce written material.

When it comes to the loss of ourselves through the loss of a significant person, being with other people who have experienced similar losses and have become new is beneficial. Wilma lost a child to an accident when the child was only five years old. She didn't think she would ever be able to live again—the best she would do was survive each day without collapsing into chaos. For many months all she could do was to put one foot in front of the other and hope it would hold her up. After about a year, she found a group of people who were all grieving the loss of a child. Some of them had a more recent loss than hers. Others had lost children ten years earlier. Walking along with these people, Wilma learned techniques to employ so she could think beyond the next moment. By being with those who had lived with loss for ten or more years, she learned that hope to live does exist. She often found it difficult to believe, but she began the ritual of attending the meetings and the practice of going out with other people.

Wilma's new way of life has recaptured some of the better dimensions of her life before her loss. She again has moments of laughter and even glimpses of joy. By forcing herself into certain disciplines of community, she has begun to see herself as a woman who has lost a child rather than simply a childless mother.

Good friends, whose presence reminds you of who you want to be, are invaluable as you move toward the new self you are becoming.

Jesus [said], "Very truly, I tell you,

no one can see the kingdom of God

without being born from above."

JOHN 3:3

10

Becoming New

ecoming a new creation is not something that you *do*. It is something that happens to you, like being born. You didn't do anything. It was a gift to you. The tenth experience of this growing-through-grieving process is a kind of birthing into a new life.

Birthing into a new life comes when you least expect it. It usually comes in fits and starts. It may start with moments when you feel comfortable being in your skin, when the driving energy you once had to run from your fears and to fill your life with frenetic activity will seem to have dissipated. You find you can sit and rest, sinking into the present moment and accept the grace of it.

This may not happen for years, but when you arrive at this stage, you will have become someone who knows joy. You know you have reached this point in the process when you feel like a child again, when you are as open to what is around you as a newborn. Rebirth does not entail coming to some way of being that you consciously choose. Rather, it is like an infant who is awake and open to all around her. An infant has not been conditioned to define some things as good and some things as bad. She is simply open to tasting and seeing, touching and discovering. You know you are becoming new when your senses and desires are once again awake and alive.

My experience with the grieving process has taught me that becoming new happens *to us*—it is not something we can create in ourselves. It comes to us when we have felt our pain, and that pain has become integrated into who we are, no longer a barrier to new experiences. It comes to us when we have remembered well what was lost and remembered long enough that it no longer defines us but simply informs who we are. It comes to us when we have experienced the grace of forgiveness, no longer being haunted by the guilt of what might have been and was not, or what was not that might have been. It comes to us when we feel strong enough to play again—to explore the larger world of strangers. It comes to us when we develop our new discoveries and find our love and our life in them.

Becoming a new creation doesn't mean we will forget the past. We will remember it as a source of understanding of who we are and who we are becoming. The past with all its pain and pleasure will have a bittersweet quality to it. The threads of memory, tinged with tears and thanksgiving, have woven themselves into a comforter, wrapping us and warming us on cold winter nights. When we awake one day and realize we are living into the present in a natural and relaxed way—not really working at it but letting it open us up to the world within and around us—we will feel a new joy and contentment. Because we feel more secure in who we have become, we can better integrate the past, present, and future. The becoming of a new self is the awareness that who we have been, who we are, and who we are becoming are no longer in painful struggle with one another. We feel whole. There will certainly be moments when emptiness will cause us to feel fractured and broken, but much of the time we will find a measure of peace.

No one can predict when this gift will come. Its arrival is usually a surprise. It comes in those moments when we feel at home in our own skin. It isn't some constant state of well-being. That kind of experience is utopia (no place). Expecting a state of nirvana always leads to disappointment. But there will be more moments of awareness that we are alive and that life is good and worth living and sharing. To be born anew in the spirit is to be alive to the living, creative spirit that breathes and moves around us.

You will know the gift of rebirth has come to you when you are able to be awake and to see the creative love of the Divine in the human and created world around you. You will have moments of delight, when your desires and your experiences marry and light shimmers in your heart.

Good Companions

The best companions when you are experiencing this dimension of becoming new are those people with whom you feel at home. These are the individuals you have met along the way who like the new person who has been born. They are folks who know how to celebrate with you as you experience joy again.

These companions may or may not include people who knew you before your loss. If they are persons who have known you before and have been able to accompany you on your journey, you are doubly blessed. For they share not only the dreams of your future but also the memories of your past. They will be there not only to walk with you in the adventure of discovering a new world, but they will be able to sit by the fire with you and remember the rich gifts of who you were before.

If the companions with you at this point are new acquaintances and have only been a part of your life since the loss, then you are richly blessed. For they respect enough of your past, which they do not know, to trust that you are who you are today because of who you have been. They have grace to accept what they do not know as a mystery that has brought them the person that they do know.

In order for us to delight in ourselves, we need the people we walk with to be those who find delight in us. The new person we have become is integrating into a new community of people who will share and celebrate that new life.

Epilogue: What Matters Most

To live is to love. To love is to lose. To lose is to live.

So where do we go from here? How do we attend to these multiple dimensions of growing and grieving? How do we stay present to the life we have and discover the new life being born within us? A few hints might give us some clues.

I was raised in a religious home with strict guidelines about behavior and belief. The stability created by a family and a social system that reinforced the beliefs was reassuring as well as stifling. Knowing what I believed helped me act with some degree of confidence.

When I went away to college, however, I lost the social system that had helped me maintain my stabilizing center. The expanding world of knowledge and the discovery that other people found different lifestyles just as satisfying as I found mine caused me to question all I held to be true and sacred. That questioning drilled through my mind and heart into the very marrow of my soul. My grieving came in the form not only of a faith crisis but also of a life crisis.

Two people helped me discern a different center to help me through the grieving process of learning to live again. The first was Bill Stringfellow, an attorney who had given up a lucrative law practice to work with the poor in Harlem, who spoke at an international youth conference I attended. Earlier in the week I had been on a boat ride on Lake Geneva in Wisconsin and had stood at the rear of the boat alone, looking down at the churning water. The black, cold chaos of the lake had seemed much calmer than the terrifying chaos of my heart and soul. I had been tempted to throw myself into the water.

I went to visit Mr. Stringfellow. I don't remember anything he said to me. I do remember receiving a package from him in the mail a few weeks after I returned to my campus in Oklahoma. I opened it and out fell a book, *Mr. Blue,* by Myles Connolly, a novel about a modern-day Saint Francis figure who gives up his inheritance to serve the poor. On the flyleaf of the book, Bill had written, "Others can be sensible, but not one who knows how few things really matter. Mr. Blue."

That book—arriving at that time in my life—enabled me to let go some of the structure and stability of my life. It helped me begin to focus on the question: What really matters? Much of what I was clinging to in order to stay afloat was mere flotsam. I needed to grieve the loss of the world I had known. I needed to open myself to the few things that mattered most for my moving ahead. But how was I to learn what really mattered?

In my quest to answer that question, I turned to one of my professors, Dr. Roger Carstensen, who taught Old Testament. I remember telling Dr. Carstensen that I didn't believe anything anymore. I was frightened and losing myself. Dr. Carstensen asked me, "Do you believe anything at all?" I thought awhile and finally said, "Well, I believe that love is better than not love." To which he said, "Faith is like a bicycle. You have to be moving to keep your balance. So if you believe in love, ride love."

Those two encounters, with people who cared enough to take me seriously and to give me the benefit of their wisdom, laid the groundwork for my whole life. I believe they laid the foundation for what matters the most when it comes to grieving loss. Riding love is the way to rediscover life through loss.

What does it mean to love? I have come to believe that love is paying attention. When you love someone, you notice him or her. You pay attention to him or her. You engage that person with your senses and your dreams, and that person becomes important to you even as he or she shapes who you are. To ride love through life is to pay attention to your life, its pain and pleasure, its joy and sorrow.

But what do we love? If only a few things really matter, what are they? As one who has found Jesus a helpful companion for life, I look to his answer. When some smart people asked him what the way to life was, he said to love God, love neighbor, and love self with all you are—heart, mind, body, and soul. That is the way of life. Pay careful attention to what is created: the environment, the neighbor, and the self. If you pay attention to this life in its multiple forms, you not only gain strength from the many relationships you have but also gain insight into how to live the life you have been given. Learning to grieve, learning to live again in the absence of something significant, isn't a matter of simply getting through some pre-ordained process. It is a matter of living fully the life you have been given as you go through it.

To love the created order, to love the neighbor, and to love the self is to pay attention to everything around you—to slow down and take notice of it—not to judge it but to see what is in it that can nourish your energy for life.

I have learned that the creation around me is filled with moments of delight and inspiration even as it is replete with terror and destruction. The problem is usually that I am so busy with all the things that matter that I fail to notice.

I was hiking in the woods recently. The trees were naked, and freshly fallen snow lay on the path. But I had important things to do, namely to raise my heartbeat so that I could do my aerobic exercise. As I exercised, I pondered the next chapter of the book I was writing, oblivious to anything around me. Then suddenly I sensed an unexpected movement off to my right. Hair standing up on the back of my neck, I stopped still to look. And there, fifty yards to the right, stood a beautiful deer—standing perfectly still, staring back at me. My heart quieted as we just gazed at each other. And I realized that here was creation, all around me; and I had almost missed it. So I slowed down as I continued on and looked at the corduroy patterns across the path as the sun shadowed through the trees. I sucked in the cold, crisp air. I allowed myself to wake up to the world around me, grateful for the sustaining environment with all its grace.

To love creation is not only to notice but also to allow oneself to be nourished by it. Deborah and I were driving through wine country in northern California. We had never been there before and we were reveling in the fertile soil and the "teddy bear" hills that rolled out ahead and behind us. We were enjoying each other and were open to the sunlight when it suddenly turned dark. We had driven into the cathedral forest of redwood trees. Towering above us were these ancient specimens of the creative hand. I pulled over, and Deborah got out of the car. I will never forget watching her walk over to one of the trees and gently place her hands on the bark and begin to weep—overwhelmed with awe at the creative life around us.

When we are broken and vulnerable, struggling to figure out who we are in the absence of someone or something significant, slowing down and taking notice of the beauty and grace around us is essential. Even the storms can serve as a reminder of the power of the unpredictable and can echo the chaos within our own souls. In the thunder and lightning of a summer storm, we can feel we are not alone in our own stormy soul.

If we are to love what God creates, then we not only pay attention to the world around us but also love our neighbor. Some people, acquaintances and strangers, inhabit all our worlds. And they are people who have value and whose perspective on life is worth listening to. Be fully present to them. This is not always an easy task. We sometimes ignore our neighbors because they are not who we want them or need for them to be. We often miss noticing the real people because we are blinded by the people we have created.

My mother has lost much of her memory, making it difficult to visit her because I don't know what to say or do. For the first ninety-one years of her life, her memory was sharp as a tack. She loved engaging issues and arguing her position. Now she cannot do that. Even while I am happy to get to "be" right now, I miss my mother. I miss her because the person I knew is not there. On a recent visit, Deborah suggested we take some recordings of hymns for my mother to listen to. (My mother was a church organist for many years and loves church music.) Deborah downloaded the hymns onto a disk; we packed up my boom box and drove the five hundred miles to visit Mother. When we got there, we saw her watching the little children who were playing at the day care center outside the window of her nursing center. So we sat with her, and while we didn't visit much, we shared her delight in the children. She waved and laughed and pointed, celebrating the child in her as she watched the children around her.

Later we went into her room and set up the CD player and began to listen to some of the great hymns of the church—"A Mighty Fortress Is Our God," "Immortal, Invisible, God Only Wise," "Great Is Thy Faithfulness," "How Great Thou Art." I sat there watching my mother, her eyes gazing at the ceiling, her fingers fluctuating between a steepled prayer and playing the organ. I heard her mouth a few of the words she could remember. I wept. For an hour, surrounded by my mother's music, my wife's grace, and pictures of my father and siblings, I wept.

I hadn't wanted to make this visit. I had important things to do. My mother was no longer there. I almost missed my neighbor. I almost missed her because she was not who I remembered her to be or wanted her to be. Had I not been there, had I not had my ego slowed down and embraced by her music, I would have missed the glimpse of my mother as a child, my mother as a poetic spirit whose soul had nurtured and cared for my soul, and who had helped shape me into who I am. [5]

To love our neighbors is to pay them our attention, to intentionally allow their gifts—as inadequate and as broken as they might feel—to embrace us. When we are frightened and lonely and struggling with our pain, we sometimes receive gifts from the most unlikely places. When we feel alone, sometimes the most wounded and scarred among us can be present in ways that offer healing to our hearts.

What matters most in our lives is to pay attention to them, to live our lives, to notice ourselves and the world around us, and to be awake to each moment, trusting that in the moment something will offer possible hope and healing.

Loving what is created also includes loving ourselves. And for many of us, loving ourself is one of the most difficult things to do. Many of us have been taught to pay attention to others and often end up ignoring our own needs. We have been taught not to be selfish, and some of us were taught to put others' needs above our own.

But loving ourselves—paying attention to our own feelings and desires—is not selfishness. Loving ourselves is realizing that creation has offered us this gift of life and the best thing we can do is to care for it in a way that allows it to live and bless others. Giving ourselves to others is hard if we do not have a self to give.

I have come to believe that self-love is not the problem in the world. Self-loathing is the problem. People who love themselves are people who rejoice in their own existence, who are strong in their own self-understanding. People who hate themselves are the ones who put others down in order to feel better about themselves. People who do not like who they are will spend all their time trying to make themselves likable. They will spend all their money trying to buy the things that will make other people like or love them. They will be easily manipulated by religious or secular leaders who want to control what they do with their lives. Self-love is discovering the gift of life you are and nurturing that gift for the sake of all of creation.

As we grieve loss and grow toward a new life, we often fail to attend to our own needs. We believe people who tell us to press on and get over it. We are often driven by our fear to stay busy so that we won't have to feel the fear. The vacancy at the table is so achingly lonely we can hardly stand it, so we keep having people over to fill the empty chair.

To be alive and to love ourselves require that we take some time just paying attention to what we are feeling and doing. In paying attention to our weariness, we might feel free to give in to it and take a rest. We may change our lives for a while to adapt to the energy it takes to rediscover our world. When I left the parish ministry and moved to the seminary, I was so exhausted with all the losses of my life that I took a nap every day in my office—lying on the floor with my feet on the chair and my head on my rolled-up jacket. To love yourself is to attend to your need in the changing landscape of your soul's journey.

As you live your life—as you live the new life emerging out of the chaos of your loss—love creation, neighbor, and self. Pay attention to what is happening around you. Notice how different you feel and search for gifts in that difference. Share your journey with strangers and friends, allowing them to offer their gifts of presence and understanding. Listen to all the new voices rising within you. Let them be heard with the other voices as well. When you do, you may discover a new self emerging within you. You may find life beyond the loss even as that life was revealed through the loss. And you may even find glimpses of peace along the way.

A DISCOVERY JOURNAL

DAN AND DEBORAH MOSELEY

This guide offers you, the reader, a journaling companion for self-discovery. It is designed as a resource to help you discover more of your life by living with the losses you have experienced. Points of personal inquiry are noted with a bullet point but you are free to write about whatever comes to mind. References to different passages in *Lose Love Live* are included in this discovery journal. You are invited to begin a journey of self-discovery by journaling about your life and your losses. We suggest using a notebook or journal to record your thoughts as it gives you the necessary room and keeps your thoughts together for reflection.

You have had many changes during your life. Life is filled with change. We change from infants to toddlers, to children, to adolescents, and so on. We also live through dozens of changes in the relationships of our lives. We also change jobs, houses, friends, beliefs, political parties, cars, schools, and partners, to name just a few. Spend a moment and list the life-changes that you can think of. Return to your list and add others as you think of them.

When changes occur, we often overlook what is lost in that change. Every change involves some loss, whether the change is chosen or not. If we chose to have children, we often focus on the gains of that change. If we choose to marry or move, we focus on the gains that occur when the change occurs. But, because of the power of the gains, we often fail to notice what has been lost. We fail to notice the lost security, the lost familiarity, and the lost companionship.

Lose Love Live defines the word *grief* as "learning to live again in the absence of something or someone significant." We become who we are by what we love. When we lose what we love, we lose a part of who we are. When we lose something (kids going off to college, death, illness, separation, divorce), it opens the space for something else. This is not to say that your new open space is not painful, as it most certainly is. But loss isn't just the time of unbearable emptiness and tears. It is the whole process of becoming a new person shaped by the memory of what is lost while not being defined by it. Loss involves knowing ourselves as persons who lose when change occurs, not as people who are losers.

Learning to live again in the absence of something or someone significant takes time and is not a linear process. It has all the switchbacks and curves of a scenic highway. Although scenic highways take more time, they are both beautiful and often scary and are thus well worth the trip.

If we ignore the losses of our lives, we lose opportunities to know more about who we are. Significant losses in life provide great occasions for discovering who you were and who you are becoming. Therefore, living with loss is important for living your life.

Chapter 1: Naming the Loss

Any kind of growth requires giving up one thing for something else. Developing clarity about the different things you give up will help free you to move toward a new life, a new sense of self you desire. To learn to live again the absence of something or someone that is gone requires that you develop the ability to name all that is lost.

That may not sound difficult at first. After all, when a spouse dies it is clear what has been lost. He or she is no longer there. But, many other losses occur as well, not all of which are so easy to name at first. There is the loss of the future, as you envisioned it. There is the loss of being a "couple" and your role as "spouse." The list goes on.

Name your significant loss (birth, death, relationship, health, job, home, etc.).

Truthfully, your loss is greater and less obvious than to name it as a single entity. The fact is that most significant losses are multilayered, and we are unable to name them immediately. In many cases, it would be overwhelming to do so.

Review the book's examples of Sue on page 34 and Helen on page 35.

Brainstorm what additional losses have grown out of your primary/ significant loss.

As your list grows, begin to notice how complex and rich your life is. These losses indicate that your primary loss has created many other losses that need to be grieved. Your list will help you see how connected you are to that which is around you and how much these things matter.

Chapter 2: Feeling Pain

When you have loved someone or something, the absence you feel when that significant person or thing is gone can be very painful. One of the reasons we feel pain after experiencing loss is the disappearance of who we know ourselves to be. Feeling the pain of any loss teaches us the truth that the loss is real. However, allowing yourself to feel the pain of your loss activates the imagination for your new life.

Pain reminds you that you are still alive. It may come and go and often visits you at times you least expect it. When you feel the pain of sadness and loneliness, know that this is a sign that you are growing stronger.

But naming your feelings is often very difficult even when you are not in pain.

Read the example of Frank on page 42 and of Helen on page 44.

What words can you think of that describe how you feel? Jot down others along the way as you think of them.

Often we seek ways to anesthetize ourselves. Our pain cries out, and we want to do anything to prevent those painful feelings. It hurts too much, so we seek to fill the hole in our heart/gut with something else. Denial, drugs, alcohol, sex, sleep, work, TV, and even a new relationship are often used for that purpose.

How have you been trying to avoid the pain? List ways you have been doing that. Pain that emerges over time helps you discern the complexities and dimensions of your loss.

Begin to notice how your feelings change from day to day or how new feelings come over time.

When you feel pain, ask yourself what other losses you may have incurred in the significant loss you are working on or remembering.

Continue naming losses during your journaling as you think of them.

Chapter 3: Anger

Anger is scary. It is full of energy and chaos. It often feels as if you are spinning out of control. Anger is, among other things, the response the body feels when it senses a threat. When you lose someone or something that has helped you know a significant portion of who you are, you feel threatened. When your identity is threatened you may also experience anxiety.

Read the example of Tom beginning on page 51.

Also, read the example of Mike on page 54.

Anger is the body's response to threat. How have you felt threatened? What makes you angry about this loss?

Who or what made you angry?

Anger is the body's energy that enables you to either strike out at what threatens you or withdraw from it. (Fight or flight.)

How did/do you react when you feel anger?

Stay in touch with your anger. Be aware of its presence and the effect it has on your moods and choices. Don't ignore it. Find means by which to express your anger that do not hurt yourself or others, such as seeking out companions with whom you can be yourself. Also, finding ways to let off steam by going to the gym, walking, biking, or engaging in some other physical activity are very helpful.

How have you expressed or managed your anger?

Chapter 4: Remembering

Learning to live again is to spend time remembering what has been lost as you try to come to terms with the absence of someone/something important to you. The reason remembering is a continuous process is that significant losses are a loss to the whole self. They affect the mind, heart, body, and soul. Your mind becomes disoriented as you orient yourselves in relationships to significant people and things. Remembering well and long helps reorganize the mind. Remembering is also the heart's way of reorganizing the shattered and scattered pieces of your life. The heart is where the affective part of your relationships is carried.

Loss is also a physical experience. In some ways, deep within the bone marrow, the body has ways of holding the pain of loss that does not require the heart or mind to participate. Remembering helps the body come to terms with the loss. Loss also reaches deep in the soul. Losses tend to strip away much of the comfort and sense of security you have constructed for yourself. To remember is the soul's way of trying to understand and know itself in relation to the forces that both hold life and threaten life. To remember, to tell the story, is the way you come to "full body" knowing.

Remembering is more than the integrative process. It is also a way of slowing down and finding rest in the familiar. Remembering allows the space to acknowledge that your loss was a real mixture of both good and bad. Creating a memorial in the mind and the heart is a way of taking control of your life again. It can serve as a pocket-sized collection of memories that you can take with you, look at and remember when you want, and then put it away. Memorials allow you to create a fresh space for new people, relationships, and a new life. Remembering that which is lost provides a way of knowing who you are.

> List all the things you can remember, good or bad, about what or who you lost.

> What stimuli cause you to remember your loss?

> What you remember about your loss helps you discover what you love about your life. It helps you know who you are by focusing you on the things that are really important to you. Consider this idea and journal about it.

> Creating a memorial of what you lost narrows down the memories by giving them a focus.

> See the example of Jane on page 64.

> How, over time, can you create a memorial remembering the heart, mind, physical, and soul elements?

> Describe your memorial.

Chapter 5: Guilt

Guilt is a dimension of being part of a responsible community. To be in that community, to live within human circles of care, requires that people take responsibility for living with one another. An example might be the roles one assumes in a marriage. That type of responsible community most often involves a division of labor. Responsibility is inherent within any community that has stability and purpose.

Guilt is the term used when someone does not fulfill his or her responsibility. *Guilt* is a term used when we do not give what we have claimed we would give. We often feel guilty because the past didn't turn out the way we had hoped. Guilt accompanies most losses. Even if we could not have done any more to prevent a loss, we feel as if we should have.

How do you feel guilty about what you lost?

What makes you feel guilty?

What do you feel responsible for?

How could you have prevented the loss?

How did you cause the loss?

Guilt isn't just limited to relationships for which we have responsibilities and power to act. Guilt sometimes afflicts those who believe that they had the power to make a difference but didn't. Guilt may also be present even if there was nothing we could have done.

Read the examples of Gary on page 71 and of Molly on page 72.

Sorting out what we are really responsible for and what we had no power to control is crucial. If we can gain an assessment of our responsibility and what real power we had to change things, then we can open ourselves to forgiveness.

What responsibilities did you have in this loss?

What areas were in your control?

What could you have done differently?

What guilt do you have over this?

Understanding guilt and processing what your responsibility and power were will help you move beyond the painful losses of your life. Identifying the guilt you feel because of what you did or did not do to contribute to the loss, or the guilt you feel over not having the power to stave off the loss, helps you discern the limits of your own humanness. Only when you realistically view your responsibilities can you realistically judge your mistakes and move forward.

Chapter 6: Forgiving

Forgiveness is not freedom from the memory of the past. We don't forgive and forget. The past is a vital part of who you are, and pain remains central to your new self-understanding. To forgive allows the memory of the loss to shape what you do with your future but not to control what you do. Forgiveness remembers what happened: it remembers the pain, and it remembers the person and their human limits. Forgiveness moves you beyond allowing that memory to define who you are and how you will live in the future, to live your full truth. Forgiving frees you from the power of the pain of the past so that you might live in the future

Reread the example of Mark on page 79.

What pain holds you to the past?

What feeling, openly acknowledged or unacknowledged, do you have toward what was lost?

What emotional words describe this process for you?

What has been lost in the past that you have to forgive?

What part does your faith play in this process?

What discoveries have you made about yourself?

Chapter 7: Gratitude

When you have remembered and named what has been lost, you begin to get in touch with things about your life for which you are grateful. Gratitude comes from the work done on forgiveness. You will know that forgiveness of others and yourself has begun when you can look at the past and find gifts for which you are grateful. Some gifts are easy to discover, and others are not so obvious. To find gratitude in the midst of loss does not diminish the value of what is lost. It simply recognizes that there are doors of discovery that open when other doors are closed.

The ability to be grateful plays a critical part of the healing process, an important piece of growing spiritually. For you to grow is to embrace reality for what it is, not simply to lament because it isn't something else. Some find joy in the new life they must create, remembering their past and being grateful for the gifts given and open to the gifts the future will hold. Others are afraid to create that new life, living in the fear that loss will visit them again. The pain of that which was lost seems to be stuck in their soul, causing fear of the future and the loss of opportunities to come. Remembering the gifts of pleasure and pain will be helpful as you open your heart to the new life emerging within you.

Read the example of Rose on page 86.

What can you name in your loss that was good?

What can you name that was not?

What new opportunities have surfaced because of the loss of what you grieve?

What is not possible?

While it isn't always easy to see the gifts in the pain of loss and while we would not have chosen to lose someone, notice what gifts come in the empty space.

What new things have your learned about yourself?

Chapter 8: Play

When you have a significant loss, you not only lose a partner, home, job, or child, you also lose your identity. You mourn the loss not only of the other but also of yourself in relationship to the other.

How has your identity changed as a result of this loss?

Who did you know yourself to be before your loss?

To become something new requires that you try on new identities. To grow spiritually is to imagine yourself as different kinds of people, to play with different ways of being in the world. You know yourself by the associations you have with self and others. You know yourself through your past, the contemporary world, the voices of the future, and those of your own soul. (Refer to Illustration 3 on page 95.)

Whose voices (from the past, present, future, and your soul) are part of how you know yourself?

What new identities have you tried?

What experiences have you had with that?

What have you learned?

Most of us listen to those voices closest to the center of the X, which we hope will create a balanced life that reinforces what we know about ourselves. When a crisis occurs, the balanced circle in the center of the X spins out of control and creates an imbalance. Voices that were the dominant voices are no longer dominant, which creates great discomfort. However, growth occurs when we begin to pay attention to voices outside that former comfortable circle of balance and equilibrium. When we begin to play with other ways of living our lives, we create the opportunity for growth.

How have you experienced this disorientation in crisis? How would you describe it?

When have you heard new voices? What quadrant of the X are they from?

Are the voices both positive and negative?

How have those voices contributed to your life so far? What adventures have you taken as a result of those new voices?

Remember that play requires grace. That disposition of generosity to ourselves and others is important. When we play, we make mistakes. When we are uncertain about who we are and our own strengths and weaknesses, we will make mistakes. We will in many ways feel like children. Forgiveness and grace are important when one is playing in new and unfamiliar territory. We must have the freedom to make mistakes without becoming our mistakes if we are going to become new and different people.

When have you received grace from others as you have learned to play with new possibilities? How has that affected you? What additional losses were you made aware of as a result of your experiences?

How have you given yourself grace as you learn a new way to be? What additional losses have you identified?

Children discover who they are becoming by playing their way into adulthood. When we have lost who we were because we lose something that we value, we have to develop the capacity to play with new possibilities.

What new things can you do now as a result of losing something of value in the past?

What have you always wanted to do that you couldn't because of your involvement with the significant thing or person you have lost?

Who helped you find the new direction or activity in your life?

What new opportunities are you exploring or enjoying as you play with new life?

Chapter 9: Practice

As you grow through grieving you will eventually understand that some options represent who you are more than others. When you come to that awareness, you can begin practicing those options more than others.

- What new options have you discovered?
- What new practices have you begun?
- What old practices have you given up to make room for the new ones?

The first thing to do when you feel you want to become the person you now imagine yourself to be is to decide—to make a choice. Without any decision, committing yourself to doing what brings new life is hard. What happens at this point in the process of grieving is that you may allow your love for what you are becoming to shape how you spend your time. As you spend more time living the role you are learning, you often grow in your love for it.

See the example of Sarah beginning on page 104.

What new life have you discovered? How is your love for what you are becoming shaping how you spend your time?

How would you describe your new life?

When the time comes on the journey of learning to live a new life, you must make a decision and begin to practice it. Mistakes may be made, but until a commitment is made, the full effect of the new direction will not be known. Only the practice of that commitment brings about the new life.

What new decisions have you made?

How are you practicing them regardless of your fear of making mistakes?

Chapter 10: Becoming New

Becoming a new person after loss is not something that you do—it is something that happens to you. It comes when you least expect it. Becoming a new person after loss is a layered experience. It comes in fits and starts. It will suddenly occur to you that you feel comfortable living in your own skin again. This may not happen for years, but when you arrive there, you will have become someone who knows joy. You will know it when you are open to what is around you again.

How far along are you in this process?

We will know that we are new when our senses and desires are awakened and alive.

Do you feel this way?

It comes to us when we have felt our pain and that pain has become integrated into who we are, not a barrier to new experiences.

Has this happened to you?

What pain still haunts you?

It comes to us when we have remembered well what was lost and long enough that it no longer defines who we are.

How is your loss defining you?

Which memories are easier to share than others?

How have you memorialized your loss?

It comes to us when we have experienced the grace of forgiveness and are no longer haunted by the guilt of what might have been.

Do you still feel guilty? If so, about what?

Where have you found forgiveness?

It comes to us when we feel strong enough to play again and explore the larger world of strangers.

What new people have you met?

Who has helped you in your grief process?

What have they helped you discern about yourself?

It comes to us when we develop our new discoveries and find our love and our new life in them.

What new discoveries have you made?

How have you made them?

What new loves do you have?

No one can say when the gift will come. Its arrival is usually a surprise. It comes in those moments when you are comfortable just with yourself. It isn't some constant state of well-being. There will be more moments of awareness that we are alive and that life is good and worth living and sharing. To be born anew in the spirit is to be alive to the living, creative spirit, which breathes and moves around us. We will know that gift of rebirth when we are able to simply be awake and see the creative love of the Divine in the human and created world around us.

Living with loss is a long, nonlinear process, much like traveling the old back roads with the twists, turns, and overlooks. As you continue to explore your new life, revisit each topic often to unearth new insights.

Blessing for the journey.

Notes

1. Susan Ford Wiltshire, *Seasons of Grief and Grace: A Sister's Story of AIDS* (Nashville, Tennessee: Vanderbilt University Press, 1994), 87.

2. *Ibid*, 88.

3. Jack Gilbert, "Tear It Down," in *The Great Fires: Poems 1982–1992* (New York: Alfred A. Knopf, 2000), 9.

4. Milan Kundera, *Immortality*, trans. Peter Kussi (New York: Perennial Classics/Harper Collins Publishers, 1999), 223.

5. My mother died August 31, 2007, during the writing of this book. The gift of her spirit that came through this experience of poetry and music will continue to sustain me.

Recommended Reading

On my journey through loss, the following books have been my good friends. In their own unique way they have given me a sense that I am not alone and that dark days are not only followed by brighter ones, but that there are gifts in the darkness.

Ackerman, Diane. *A Natural History of the Senses*. Magnolia, MA: Peter Smith Publisher, 2002.

Attig, Thomas. *How We Grieve: Relearning the World*. New York: Oxford University Press, 1996.

Bridges, William. *Transitions: Making Sense of Life's Changes*. New York: Basic Books, 2004.

Cousineau, Phil. *The Art of Pilgrimage: The Seeker's Guide to Making Travel Sacred*. Collingdale, PA: DIANE Publishing, 2003.

Dillard, Annie. *Pilgrim at Tinker Creek*. New York: Harper Perennial, 2007.

Farley, Wendy. *The Wounding and Healing of Desire: Weaving Heaven and Earth*. Louisville, KY: Westminster John Knox Press, 2005.

Holmes, Barbara Ann. *Joy Unspeakable: Contemplative Practices of the Black Church*. Minneapolis, MN: Augsburg Fortress Publishers, 2004.

Lane, Belden. *The Solace of Fierce Landscapes: Exploring Desert and Mountain Spirituality*. New York: Oxford University Press, 2007.

Moffat, Mary Jane, ed., *In the Midst of Winter: Selections from the Literature of Mourning.* New York: Knopf Doubleday Publishing, 1992.

Sittser, Jerry. *A Grace Disguised: How the Soul Grows through Loss.* Grand Rapids, Michigan: Zondervan, 2009.

Taylor, Barbara Brown. *When God Is Silent.* Cambridge, MA: Cowley Publications, 1998.

de Waal, Esther. *Living with Contradiction: An Introduction to Benedictine Spirituality.* Harrisburg, PA: Morehouse Publishing, 1998.

Weems, Renita J. *Listening for God: A Minister's Journey through Silence and Doubt.* New York: Simon and Schuster, 2000.

Weil, Simone. *Waiting for God.* New York: Harper Perennial, 2009.

Whyte, David. *The Heart Aroused: Poetry and the Preservation of the Soul in Corporate America.* New York: Knopf Doubleday Publishing, 1996.

Wiltshire, Susan Ford. *Seasons of Grief and Grace: A Sister's Story of AIDS.* Nashville, TN: Vanderbilt University Press, 1994.